DATE DUE

Scientific Selling

CREATING HIGH-PERFORMANCE SALES TEAMS THROUGH APPLIED PSYCHOLOGY AND TESTING

NANCY MARTINI
with GEOFFREY JAMES

WILEY

John Wiley & Sons, Inc.

Published by John Wiley & Sons, Inc., Hoboken, New Jersey.
Published simultaneously in Canada.

For general information on our other products and services or for technical support, please contact our Customer Care Department within the United States at (800) 762-2974, outside the United States at (317) 572-3993 or fax (317) 572-4002.

Wiley publishes in a variety of print and electronic formats and by print-on-demand. Some material included with standard print versions of this book may not be included in e-books or in print-on-demand. If this book refers to media such as a CD or DVD that is not included in the version you purchased, you may download this material at http://booksupport.wiley.com. For more information about Wiley products, visit www.wiley.com.

Library of Congress Cataloging-in-Publication Data:

Martini, Nancy, 1959-
  Scientific selling : creating high-performance sales teams through applied psychology and testing / Nancy Martini with Geoffrey James.
    p. cm.
  Includes bibliographical references.
  ISBN 978-1-118-16797-7 (cloth); ISBN 978-1-118-22641-4 (ebk); ISBN 978-1-118-23960-5 (ebk); ISBN 978-1-118-26429-4 (ebk)
  1. Selling—Psychological aspects. 2. Success in business. I. James, Geoffrey, 1953- II. Title.
  HF5438.8.P75M32 2012
  658.8'102—dc23

                                                           2011046751

Printed in the United States of America
10 9 8 7 6 5 4 3 2 1

This book is dedicated to Steve Satin, my husband, best friend, and biggest fan, and to our combined five kids—Mark, Lindsay, Allison, Ben, and Ashley—I love you all.

Contents

Acknowledgments

T his book reflects the effort and support of many people who were both directly and indirectly involved in making this book come to life.

At the top of the list to acknowledge is my coauthor Geoffrey James, who helped bring our joint vision to life with endless hours of writing, editing, interviewing, and guidance. A colleague and friend, we often joke about "thinking alike" and the book is evidence that it is so. Thank you for all your hard work and wise insights.

A big thanks to my agent Lorin Rees of the Rees Agency in Boston, he is a pleasure to work with and made the entire experience seamless. From phone calls to sharing pizza, his sage advice was always welcome.

A special thanks to my editor Dan Ambrosio of John Wiley & Sons, Inc., for his initial call and all the interim conversations to get the book launched, for driving to NYC to meet for coffee to answer my endless list of questions, and for all the ongoing support, an awesome professional.

Within the PI Worldwide offices in Wellesley, there is a wonderful group of people who contributed either directly on content or indirectly in putting up with me during this process. I'd like to acknowledge Todd Harris, PhD, for his help in reading sections of the book and contributing his valuable input as needed. I'm thankful to Cindy Lynes for being there when the book idea was "born" and supplying Geoffrey with various materials along the way, and to her marketing team of Tara Kelley, Anna Dreyser, and Sarah Messer for all the fun they will have promoting the book. I'd like to recognize Judy Olivo for booking interviews, scheduling meetings, and for keeping people out of my office and keeping me in. Although behind the scenes now, my friend and past CFO of PI Worldwide, Mike Giarratano, is an ongoing source of straight talk and no nonsense thinking. A big thanks to Frank Hunnewell, our COO, for taking charge and helping to run the company, without you this book could not have happened.

I'd like to acknowledge the PI Worldwide staff members who work hard every day to bring the science of the PI and the SSAT to the world, in no particular order: the Technology team with Thomas Zacharia, Chris Pecorella, Calton Chakwizira, Bob Comisky, John French, Bob Schiebel, and Harry Moulis; the Finance team led by Joe Rossi, VP of Finance, Lorraine Rawson, Steve Sharp, Lisa Cooper, Sue Flanagan, Mike King, and Samantha Ellinwood; the Administrative team with Arlene Smith and Cathy McGrath; the Legal team with Mary Beth Cotter and the Science team with Claire Rickards; Helen Hailer, our HR Director; the PI Worldwide University team with Paula Silva; and finally the Sales Team, who not only provide these tools to their clients but also live the science of selling: Rooney Russell, Kathleen Teehan, and from the original Global Sales Alliance team—Megan Holsinger.

Along with our corporate team, the global network of PI Worldwide licensees and consultants around the world were instrumental in helping with client interviews and data for this book. It is my pleasure to first acknowledge those who were interviewed: Dave O'Brien, Kathleen Teehan, Dave Lahey, Mike Stewart, Doug McCann, and Jennifer Mackin. I would also like to recognize the licensees in this network that help bring client results every day with the PI in 62 languages active in 143 countries around the world:

Antonio Aguelo

Hamed Al Tamami

Robert Berg

Bob Clark

Nancy Clark

Pat Conway

Dan Courser

Steve Cundall

Venkatesh Desai

Patrice Donohue and Susan Mask

Jack Evans

Robert Ferrara

Kathy Frank

Larry Good

Scott Greenwood

Erik Herman

Tony High

Doug Johnson

Axel Knudsen

Stan Kulfan

David Lahey

Scott Lappin

Jennifer Mackin

George McColgan

Chuck Mollor

Hock Chong Oh

Elmano Nigri

Steve Picarde

Helene Rodrigue

Meg Roy of Lurie Besikof Lapidus & Company

David Schwartz

Rick Sobotka of Meaden & Moore

Mike Stewart

Montse Sugranes

Rich Sweeney

Ben Venter

Doug Waggoner

Chantal Walley

Steve Waterhouse

Bob Wilson and Heather Haas

David Wiseman

Robin Wood and Tommy Kennedy Bartshukoff

Jeff Wulf and Jim Klunick of WIPFLI

Jessy Yu

These licensees are supported by an incredible team of 350 consultants around the world, and although I cannot list them all here, the Top 20 globally must be recognized—kudos to each one for the dedication and results they create daily for their clients: Ruedi Affentranger and Stephanie Affentranger Kveton, PI Europe; Morten Løkkegaard, PI Europe; Fiona Brookwell, PI Europe; Rooney Russell, PI Worldwide; Michael Kirk-Jensen, PI Europe; Freidemann Stracke, PI Europe; Dave O'Brien, Predictive Group; Michael Wohl, The Oliver Group; Vic Coppola, P.I. Associates; Dave Osborne, Predictive Success; John Ranalleta, ADVISA; Mike Maynard, Predictive Group; Kathleen Teehan, PI Worldwide; Marc Aubé-Chousseaud, PI Europe; Steve Caldwell, Predictive Group; Nelien Krijtenburg, PI Europe; Scott Kiefer, The Oliver Group; Jim Klunick, WIPFLI; Jim Jones, PI Midwest; and Steve Picarde Jr., PI Midlantic.

I'd also like to acknowledge the thousands of sales reps that I have taught over the years at Global Sales Alliance and the hundreds of clients and consultants I had the honor of working with. Many have become lifelong friends and colleagues. A special thanks to Robert Burnside, Ray Kotcher, Kelley Skoloda and all the fine folks at Ketchum, Dave DeFillipo, Lisa Shapiro, Christi Pedra, Nancy Leeser, Nadia Altomare, Joe Riley, Bill Roche, Donna Thaxter, Bruce Liebowitz (in memory), Nancy Weeks, Gary Caine, Nancy Michaels, Stephen Carr, and last but not least—Jeb Bates, longtime consultant, colleague, and friend. After years of traveling the sales circles, I want to recognize my esteemed colleagues who carry a strong voice in the industry—Dave Stein of ES Research, Gerhard Gschwandtner of *SellingPower* and his wonderful daughter Larissa Gschwandtner—for the many fine discussions on sales and the future of selling.

For years I was part of a mastermind group and many of those days were spent brainstorming with colleagues about sales, strategy, and sales performance; to the original Global Sales Alliance team—I'd like to acknowledge Bob Frare, Ed Robinson, and Steve Waterhouse, proof that competitors working together can make one plus one equal three.

There is a special place in my heart for the Daniels family and our board of directors, for their dedication to behavioral science, the commitment to grow this fine company, and the confidence in turning over the reins to a professional management team. A special tribute in memory of Arnold Daniels (founder) and Dinah Daniels (daughter and past President and CEO) for their contribution to scientific selling and the opportunity to carry this fine company forward—they are missed. To Sally Daniels and Elisabeth Daniels DePristo for believing in the future of PI Worldwide, caring about this company and all the people in it, and allowing us to embrace growth with a passion. I'd like to acknowledge and thank our PI Worldwide board members—Ed Neville, attorney, the voice of reason and always a willing ear; Mike Roberts, our longest serving board member, bringing experience and insight to the table; Frank Haydu, a much appreciated mentor and friend. I sincerely appreciate the full support you all gave to this project.

I think I have been selling since I was about three years old and must thank my father Bill Martini for his invaluable early lessons on sales and life that certainly led to the philosophies in this book. In recognition of my mother, Ginny Martini, for being an incredible mother and friend, always there to cheer me on. Much of my early education came from being the baby of the family, I learned how to get things by persuasion—a big hug and thank you to my siblings for the opportunities to learn on them—Barbara Bardsley, Donald Martini, Steven Martini, Richard Martini, and Sue Martini.

Finally, I am deeply grateful to be married to the man of my dreams, Steve Satin, who brought laughter and joy back into my life. And for my two children Mark and Allison who make me proud every day, and to my three stepchildren who I am honored to know and love, Lindsay, Ashley, and Ben. You are all what makes my world go round.

Foreword

Very few people in the world of business understand what selling is all about. In fact, there's a historical prejudice against salespeople and the act of selling that goes back decades.

When I was a computer programmer in the 1980s, everyone in engineering thought the sales guys were glad-handers whose only talent consisted of an unending ability to schmooze. We were *absolutely certain* our technology was so manifestly wonderful that the only useful function the sales team could provide was to show the customers where to sign on the dotted line.

Ironically, what our sales guys were selling were million-dollar computer systems at the beginning of the PC revolution. Those guys were heroes, as evidenced by the fact that they actually were capable of making any sales at all. And yet, I'm embarrassed to say that we engineers treated them like they were bozos.

Some things never change. The other day, I was sharing a ride with an unemployed programmer. When I explained that I now wrote about sales and selling, she said, and I quote: "I think sales guys are slimy." I could, of course, have mounted a spirited defense of the profession but instead I just said: "Hey, now you know why your company went out of business."

That shut her up. Wish somebody had done the same to me, back in the day.

However, it's not like engineering types have the market cornered on prejudice against sales folk. After I got out of engineering, I worked in the marketing group for a Fortune 50 corporation. And, guess what? The marketers were just as dismissive of sales professionals as the engineers had been.

Over a six-year period, I watched (and helped) that marketing group spend over a hundred million dollars on (1) brochures that nobody read, (2) videos that nobody watched, (3) incomprehensible market research reports, and (4) presentations full of biz-blab and arrant gobbledegook.

While we were wasting money like it had an expiration date, we marketers chortled among ourselves about how naive and silly the sales guys were. The phrase we used was "marketing drives sales" as if we were somehow in control, and the sales team were order-taking mules that would go wherever we pointed them.

I wince whenever I remember how I thought back then.

Here's the truth. The only reason that company was surviving was that the sales guys were cutting HUGE deals for highly customized hardware, software, and services. It was incredibly complex stuff to sell . . . and their job was made *even more difficult* by the fact that they had to explain away the nonsense coming out of the marketing group.

I wish I could say that kind of thing didn't happen anymore. But I can't.

Every time I explain in my sales blog that "strategic marketing" is an oxymoron, I get dozens of whiney comments from marketing professionals, sometimes using the actual phrase: "marketing drives sales." Those guys are as clueless as I ever was and the sales guys who have to work with them have my deepest sympathies.

Now, you'd think that top executives wouldn't be as dumb as engineers and marketers. But you'd think wrong.

Over the past decade, I've interviewed dozens of top executives and when the subject of sales and selling comes up, the vast majority held the same kind of distorted opinions.

I've heard CEOs of billion-dollar companies say stuff like: "I have no idea what goes on in the sales group." I once heard a CFO blather for 15 minutes about how much his sales team was spending on their expense account, an amount that turned out to be less than .1 percent of the revenue they were creating. Incredible.

Ludicrous, isn't it?

Consider: The entire business world, indeed the entire system of global capitalism, is entirely dependent upon sales professionals. (Even a mass-market consumer retail product has a supply chain that requires dozens of sales reps.) And still, they "can't get no respect."

If you look around, you see people at all levels of most corporations who (best case) are scratching their heads and wondering what the sales team actually does or (worst case) actively treating their sales professionals as persona non grata.

Needless to say, all this confusion and rancor does not make it easier to sell. Quite the contrary. In my experience, these antisales attitudes are most predominant inside companies that are about to fail. The companies that survive and thrive, especially in hard times, have corporate cultures that deeply respect the sales function.

Unfortunately, such companies often seem to be few and far between.

Ever since I've been writing about sales and selling, I've discussed this perception problem with dozens of sales gurus and trainers. Their reaction varied from "that's just how it is" to "people will come around when the numbers go up."

Yeah, right.

It wasn't until I interviewed Nancy Martini that I got an answer that made sense. She said: "The reason sales teams don't get respect is that companies measure the wrong things."

It's not that sales teams weren't being measured. It was that the metrics (like revenue and conversion rates) weren't granular enough to be useful in creating sales teams or in explaining the "why" behind sales performance. It's like measuring grains of sand with a yardstick. Yeah, you can do it, but it doesn't give you any actionable data.

The lack of actionable metrics meant that selling was condemned to remain a "black box" that nobody understood. And when people don't understand something, it creates fear, doubt, and misunderstanding. And that's why sales gets a bad rap.

Scientific selling (the concept, not the book) changes all of that.

Scientific selling makes it both possible and practical to measure potential, train teams and individuals precisely, and measure the results. Scientific selling not only makes sales teams better able to make the big metrics (which is obviously still essential), but it also makes it easier for sales managers to explain to the rest of the company what sales is all about.

More importantly, scientific selling reveals the truth that's been hidden for so long, which is that selling is a specialized skill that can only be done by certain types of people, and deserves the respect of *everyone* in *every* company.

In short, the solution to the image problem is a heavy dose of science.

That's why I'm excited about this book and about my participation in making it happen. Nancy is pioneering something that is, and will continue to, change the culture of selling and how the world perceives it.

And that's huge.

—Geoffrey James

Preface

I love selling. Everything about it works—it's interesting, captivating, challenging, strategic, and you are measured every day. Today you have to be good to make it in sales.

Along with my interest in selling, I've always been profoundly curious as to why some people succeed in sales and others don't. That's why I'm a convert to the scientific approach to selling. Science provides exciting insight and concrete answers to predictable sales performance.

By "scientific," I'm not talking about pseudoscience or laying a gloss of scientific-sounding words over the same old folk wisdom that's been pushed in sales training courses for the past century and a half.

I'm talking about hard science—a quantitative, statistically valid measurement of human behavior, making changes in that behavior, and remeasuring the results. I'm talking about actual mathematics, and PhD-level research.

I didn't always feel this way. Time was that I thought selling was pretty much all about the art of making the sale.

This book is a manifesto for the scientific approach to selling. But it's also a story about how I made the transition to a scientific worldview and how that transition has impacted my work life and my ability to sell.

By the time I started college I knew that I wanted to be in sales. I tried to sit still for business classes, but I couldn't help thinking that I ought to be out there selling something. So, like many salespeople before me, I left academia after two years in order to start doing what I knew I was fated to do: sell.

And, just to test myself and my resolve, I picked an industry that's one of the most difficult and demanding: life insurance. I figured that "if I can make it there, I can make it anywhere."

The company that hired me represented exactly what everyone hates about the sales profession. My sales manager, for example, spent the Monday morning sales meeting telling us that we were idiots and yelling at us to make bigger numbers. The sales training consisted of a series of tricks designed to manipulate people to say "yes" even if they had no fit for our product.

I remember sitting there, listening to that derogatory nonsense, and simply thinking—are you kidding me? I also noticed that the company was losing about 90 percent of its sales team every year, so I figured that if I wanted to be successful, I should probably go out and do the exact opposite of what we were being told to do.

Our group was supposed to go to college campuses and sell policies to students, using the techniques that they taught us. I figured, however, that students had a limited need or affordability for insurance, so I talked to students about the life insurance needs of their parents.

That got me lots of introductions to people who really DID need life insurance protection for their families. So there I was, all of 22 years old, selling life insurance to parents in their fifties who were making more in a week than I would make that year.

But the age difference didn't matter because I believed in the product and truly believed that the parents really needed it. And the parents didn't really care that I was the same age as their kids because I knew my product and understood what they needed, and why.

So that was my first big lesson in sales as an adult—that selling isn't about tricks and techniques, it's about understanding people's needs and figuring out how to satisfy them.

Needless to say, I'm not the first (or the last) to make that discovery, but it turns out that this realization is the foundation of scientific selling, because *if you apply science to the wrong behaviors, you'll get the wrong results.*

Not that the insurance company ever figured that out. Quite the contrary, they kept flogging those tired old techniques, with only the vaguest sense that they weren't very effective. Meanwhile, they suffered a huge turnover, and an incredible amount of lost productivity.

After completing my first full year in insurance, I was the National Rookie of the Year among a group of over 150 sales reps across the nation. Imagine, though, how different the situation would have been if they had been able to measure what I was doing, and what the handful of other highly effective reps were doing.

And imagine that the insurance company had possessed a way to implement the same behaviors more widely, and then remeasure to confirm that these new techniques were proving effective.

There's no question in my mind that that insurance company would today dominate the entire industry.

After I sold insurance for a while, I looked around for another challenge. I decided that after trying to sell something intangible, like insurance, I'd like a chance to sell something tangible. So I went to work for an alarm company.

As many sales professionals know, selling tangibles (like alarms) is a fundamentally different kind of activity than selling something that can't be held, touched, or felt.

With intangibles, you're always selling a solution and you have a lot of latitude about how you craft it. With tangibles, there's always a danger of your product becoming a commodity, in which case, the only wiggle room you have is price. And selling the lowest price is a recipe for low margins and price wars.

Since my experience was in selling a completely different kind of product, it wasn't surprising that my new employer felt strongly that I needed to move slowly and learn a lot before I actually tried to make a sale. After all, my new employer had seen plenty of new hires fail, and he didn't want to cope with another expensive failure.

The head of this company believed strongly that, in order to sell tangibles, you need to emphasize the features that make your product better. He therefore expected me to spend three months getting trained on all the product features, spending time with the installers, going along on sales calls with a seasoned sales rep, and so forth.

But the truth is, I was actually ready to sell the product right from the get-go.

On my second week, I drove past a local restaurant that I could see was being remodeled. I pulled my car over, went inside, asked for the manager and said, "You're tearing up the walls, so this is a good time to consider putting in an alarm system."

The restaurant manager said his main worry was passing inspection. So I called one of the installers, had him come over and see what needed to be done, and the manager wrote me a check.

The next day I went into the CEO's office and told him I made my first sale. He said, "No, you didn't" and proceeded to explain that I couldn't possibly know enough about the product to sell it.

Then I handed him the check. As he stared at it, I explained that alarm systems aren't about electronics and features, they're about peace of mind. That manager wanted peace of mind that his restaurant would pass inspection. And he was willing to pay for that peace of mind.

Now, I intuitively understood that because I'd been dealing with peace of mind issues in my previous job. However, my new employer had no way of seeing that, and instead, had hired me hoping I had potential. Hoping. He had no way whatsoever to discover whether or not I had what it takes.

What's worse, he didn't even know himself what attributes were required to be successful selling alarms. He thought it was all about being technically savvy and being able to talk about features and functions. The real requirement was more along the lines of what I had aplenty: an ability to make people feel secure that they're making the right decision.

My new boss could have saved himself a lot of bother if he had just been able to measure my abilities from the start and compare them to other successful sales professionals in that field. He would have quickly discovered that, when selling peace of mind, being product savvy, while important, was far less important than being people savvy.

As I continued in my sales career, I started networking at local Chamber of Commerce meetings. One day, a CEO came over to me and said, "I notice that your sales volumes are crazy high and I don't understand how you do that. Can you give me some advice?"

I wasn't terrifically interested in mentoring a CEO, but we ended up having lunch and he brought up a couple of situations that were in his pipeline. I gave him some pointers, and he was so impressed that he asked if he could pay me to do more. He also said he had some CEO friends who could use my help with sales advice.

I told him "Thanks, but I already have a job," but later, when I got a chance to think about it, it occurred to me that it might actually be fun to do sales consulting and sales training and it would give me the opportunity to impact more businesses and more people.

I founded a company called NetWorks, and began teaching networking skills and lead generation. That quickly evolved into a more comprehensive sales training program that addressed all the steps in the sales process and eventually became Global Sales Alliance. The business grew rapidly, moving quickly from regional, to national, to international.

However, while I knew I was teaching valuable techniques, there was this nagging feeling that it wasn't always as effective as it could be. The process of selling was easy to teach but I was limited in the amount of data I had about the sales reps and their ability to execute on the knowledge. It became clear to me that different sales reps found the "Customer-Focused Selling" (which is what the training eventually evolved into) either difficult to execute or easy to execute, depending on their basic personality.

That's where scientific selling first came into my view of the sales world.

One of my favorite clients in the early days was a company called PI Worldwide, publisher of the Predictive Index (PI) since 1955. After working with them briefly I said, "every one of my clients needs this PI thing to understand their sales reps, why would anyone function without it?"

My clients that used the PI had huge business results including reducing turnover and increasing sales revenue. Clients were using PI to assess the character traits of new hires and existing employees. After I was trained in the PI system, I found that I could predict who would be most likely to implement CFS by looking at their PI results. I therefore found myself frequently recommending the PI to my clients.

Even so, I noticed that behavioral assessment wasn't always enough. I ran across some cases that had a compatible PI profile for sales, but who didn't seem willing or able to actually perform the specific skills that would increase their sales performance. I therefore decided this was an area ripe for research, and worked with an expert to devise a way to test for the specific skills that were required to sell effectively.

And that was the genesis of the Selling Skills Assessment Tool (SSAT).

My company, which at that point consisted of about eight trainers, had great synergy with the products of PI Worldwide because the behavioral and skills measure was a unique power pack for managing sales growth. This was firm proof that selling can be, and should be, measured scientifically.

To make a long story short, PI Worldwide acquired my company in 2006 and I became CEO in 2007. Today, PI Worldwide is the premier firm that uses scientific behavior and skills data to measure and drive sales performance.

Despite the success of PI Worldwide in the marketplace, this book is NOT an introduction to the company's products. While they're used as examples, this book deals with the science that lies behind them, and how that science can be applied to selling, regardless of the specific assessment tools that are actually used.

The shift toward scientific selling and away from the mystical and anecdotal concept of what selling is all about is, in my view, the most significant development in selling over the past decade, even during a period of history that has seen massive changes in nearly every aspect of the selling.

It's not that scientific selling has had an enormous impact, yet. While there are hundreds of companies practicing it, they're just the tip of a proverbial iceberg. The real impact of scientific selling will occur when it's the rule, rather than the exception.

This book looks forward to that day.

1

The Science of Selling

We are focusing on cultural and structural change because our business is growing and changing all the time, and the economy has forced some changes and we're expecting more in the future. Our business used to be a low-level sale, and we had a "one sales style fits all" philosophy. Over time, though, there emerged many different customer types, who wanted to interact with us in different ways. As a result, we've had to change the way managers recruit and design their team, all based upon a better understanding of the work that needs to be done.
—Shane McCarrey, Manager of Human Relations and Development, ABS Global

This book is about the application of science to the business of selling. There are many other books about selling that have "science" in their titles. However, in every case that we've examined, the science was simply that: part of the title. The term was tacked onto the title in order to give those books some borrowed credibility, even though they were full of the same "how I sold a million-dollar deal in a day" anecdotes that are, unfortunately, common to the genre.

By "science," we mean real science that is based on gathering observable, empirical, and measurable evidence and analyzing that evidence according to specific, generally accepted principles of reasoning and logic. We mean real science that follows the scientific method, consisting of the collection of data through experimentation, and the formulation and testing of hypotheses. In this book we are emphatically *not* going to discuss pseudosciences that require a huge dollop of faith in order to be believed.

This book is also a manifesto for the scientific approach to selling. It contains numerous case studies of how that scientific approach has helped companies and shows *exactly* how the application of *real* science improves everything in the sales environment—from management to coaching to training to creating long-term sustainable sales results. It also describes how the further application of new areas of scientific inquiry, like neuroscience and cognitive science, will further change the business of selling.

The Changing Nature of Selling

This scientific revolution in sales and sales process is taking place in the midst of the most extensive transformation of the role of sales managers, teams, and individuals in the history of business. For decades, the role of sales rep remained static. Sales reps provided information to customers and wrote up orders, greasing the wheels of commerce with a hefty dollop of schmooze.

That began to change around 2002, as the Internet (following the dot-com era of experimentation) started to become an integral part of the business landscape. A series of new technologies, ranging from e-mail to automated supply chains to cloud computing to smartphones to web conferencing to search engines to social media, were thrust into the workplace. While some of these technologies existed previously, the Internet freed their disruptive potential, which has rippled through every aspect of the modern corporation.

Nowhere has the transformation been more significant than in the way that companies buy and sell from each other, and sell to consumers. So much has changed, in fact, that it's probably impossible to enumerate everything that's different from just 10 years ago. However, we believe that the following trends represent the highlights of this massive set of changes:

Trend 1: Buyers Have More Information. Today's buyers already have more information at their fingertips online than was imaginable even 10 years ago. In a matter of seconds, prospects can discover a wealth of information about a company, its competition, and its industry. Buyers aren't limited to hard data and can also gather soft data from friends, colleagues, and strangers (e.g., anonymous reviews) on social media sites. In other words, buyers have the potential to be better educated and theoretically to make better decisions.

Trend 2: Selling Is More Demanding. As more people have used the Internet as their first stop and social media simultaneously, the sales roles are evolving to match, if only because there is less tolerance for old-school selling and tactics. To be successful, today's sales professionals must possess all the core sales skills of a top consultant, the intelligence to assimilate information rapidly, the behavioral fit to excel under pressure, the stamina to draw upon the resilience needed in this field, and the wisdom to facilitate the sales process rather than sell in the old sense of "doing something to" the prospect.

Trend 3: Buyers Are More Risk-Averse. As the economy has become more unpredictable, customers have become understandably more conservative about spending money, instituting new controls and review processes that make it more difficult for spending to take place. When customers "hunker down" in this manner, the new reviewers are frequently drawn from the ranks of top management, thereby transferring authority away from the operational staff (with whom a sales professional is most likely to be familiar) and putting it into the hands of a more remote group of executives. Such stakeholders are inherently more difficult to contact, are more likely to have gatekeepers that deflect sales professionals, and are more likely to look askance at sales professionals.

Trend 4: Selling Is Becoming More Professional. The number of business schools offering courses in sales is rapidly increasing and sales professionals are more likely to get MBAs or other kinds of business training than in the past. While most sales positions today do not require a degree or some form of professional certification, there is certainly a trend toward the kind of specialization that, in other jobs (like the practice of medicine in the early twentieth century), has led toward the creation of a professional class.

Trend 5: Inside Sales Teams Are Growing. While the "road warrior" remains a cultural stereotype both inside and outside the business world, there has been a continuous shift from outside sales to inside sales in terms of how companies deploy their sales resources. According to a recent survey conducted by Dr. James Oldroyd (formerly of MIT and now at the Korean business school SKK GSB), corporate hiring of outside sales reps over the past few years has leveled off at a .5 percent annual growth, while hiring of inside sales reps is growing at a lively 7.5 percent annual clip.

Trend 6: Sales and Marketing Are Merging. The long-term battle between sales and marketing is drawing to a close because technology is cutting off the root of the conflict, which has always been differences of opinion over what constitutes a good lead. Lead generation tools from websites to search engines (combined with a wealth of information on the Web) make it possible to track the effectiveness of marketing's contribution through the sales cycle. Sales and marketing teams are forced to work together to make the numbers go up without recourse to fingerpointing.

Trend 7: Selling Is Becoming More Global. Sales teams must now balance cultural and regional realities from social norms to language. Working with a global team of colleagues and a global client increases the complexity and the challenge of group decision making on both sides. Sales professionals must now have knowledge and experience in "world selling," not simply those practices that work in their own geographical region. This drives a higher reliance on sophisticated selling techniques, rather than traditional tactics that worked when selling was a more localized activity.

Trend 8: Increased Use of Social Media. Social media provides a rep with access to a breadth of knowledge about key decision makers. A rep can use social media to find a senior decision maker's name, gather professional and personal data, check other business contacts to track current connections, and then put all the pieces together to formulate a strategic approach to penetrating and developing the account. Sales managers utilize social media sites to find new sales reps, both those actively job hunting and those merely contemplating a move.

Trend 9: Sales Teams Are Pioneering New Technology. In decades past, sales teams were somewhat of a technological backwater. Today, they're usually the first group to embrace new technology. For example, Customer Relationship Management (CRM) was the killer application that made the cloud computing concept more than just an academic theory. Sales reps have also been the earliest adopters of smartphones and tablet computers and, in their search for more convenient ways to connect, have led the growth in web conferencing and social media.

In other words, just about everything in the world of selling is changing. Unfortunately, many sales managers often find it difficult or impossible to keep atop of these changes and to use them to their advantage.

Instead, they continue to cling to hiring practices, sales processes, and compensation plans that actively discourage top sales professionals from ever achieving their potential in today's more complex selling environment.

The Crisis in Sales Management

The world economy, of course, has been extremely challenging since 2008, experiencing one of the worst recessions of modern times, followed by years of weak growth and scant demand for goods and services. Not surprisingly, many sales teams are struggling.

For example, the market research firm CSO Insights recently surveyed over 2,800 companies worldwide to assess their current level of sales performance, the challenges facing sales teams today, and how companies were effectively dealing with those issues. The survey discovered that in 2009 the percentage of reps making quota stood a measly 51.8 percent, down from 58.8 percent in the previous year. In other words, nearly half of all sales reps were failing, even though sales management was presumably adjusting their quotas in order to match their expected selling potential.

Since the overall business environment and economy is not going to change, the onus is upon sales management and sales teams to adapt to these new and challenging conditions. Unfortunately the delta between where most sales organizations are today and where they need to be in the future is enormous and growing.

When surveyed, sales managers are not at all sanguine about their ability to effectively field sales teams. Most sales managers estimate that only 40 percent to 60 percent of their current sales professionals are prepared to execute even the basic trusted advisor sales strategies, according to Todd Harris, a PhD who works for the leadership development and sales effectiveness firm PI Worldwide.

There's also growing evidence that the old 80/20 rule (80 percent of your revenue comes from 20 percent of the sales staff) is becoming even more dichotomous. Sales guru Mike Bosworth, for example, regularly cites research showing that, on average, almost 87 percent of most companies' revenue comes from the top 13 percent of a company's sales performers.

What's developing is what might be called a "million-dollar gap" between the best and the rest, with many organizations struggling to find emerging sales leaders, even while trying to get the most out of the personnel that they already have. While most sales managers understand the value of sharing best practices, they often have only a vague idea of why one sales professional can successfully sell five times as much as the person in the next office, using the same sales process and sales tools to sell the exact same product.

Part of the problem is the ad-hoc procedures that most firms use to hire their sales professionals. According to CSO Insights, only four in ten firms systematically assess the basic competency of their sales candidates. Almost half of the firms surveyed felt that their ability to "hire the right sales professionals" needed improvement, but only a measly 11 percent were planning to alter their hiring process.

Slapdash hiring creates unstable organizations that are constantly losing talent before their promise can be fulfilled. Astoundingly, annual sales representative turnover rates average approximately 30 percent, which means that one out of three sales professionals is likely to leave the typical organization every year. Since that's the average, many sales organizations suffer from attrition rates that are far higher.

This high rate of turnover creates a constant need for replacement personnel. Most companies report that it takes six months or longer to ramp up a new sales representative to full productivity. That figure is just for the average sales professional; fully replacing a top sales professional could easily take longer, if such replacement is even possible. The situation with sales management is even worse. According to *SellingPower* magazine, the average tenure for a CSO or VP of Sales is now less than two years, barely long enough for the new executive to learn the ropes and begin to have an impact.

This constant personnel churn costs money—right at a time when companies are, due to the economy, most concerned about savings. General estimates vary but the rule of thumb is that turnover costs typically run anywhere between one and a half to two and a half times a person's base salary. Part of that is direct costs (such as the cost of recruitment), but in the case of sales professionals can include additional costs, such as loss of customers, loss of contact information, and loss of credibility in customer accounts.

Difficult economic times are challenging for sales managers. Opportunities become scarce as prospects stop spending. Increased competition for a shrinking base of customers makes revenue harder to generate and it becomes more difficult to keep reps engaged and motivated. This can make it difficult to keep top sales employees, who are likely to look for employment in companies and industries where sales have become less scarce.

Conversely, an improving economy can also create retention problems. Employees become less concerned with job security and more concerned with advancing their careers, even if that means finding employment elsewhere. Indeed, according to a recent survey conducted by the accounting firm Deloitte LLP, fully one-third of employed Americans plan to look for a new job as the economy improves.

Regardless of economic conditions, sales professionals are especially likely to leave, according to Dave Stein, CEO of ES Research, a firm that measures and analyzes sales training.

"Eight to ten years ago, if a salesperson worked at several companies for less than three or four years, they'd be considered unreliable," he explains. "Today, especially in fast-moving markets, salespeople are expected to have experience in multiple firms, selling to multiple industries."

To make matters worse, the employees most likely to leave are the younger workers who have the potential to be future leaders, according to a recent survey conducted by the Opinion Research Corporation. While so-called "baby boomers" (aged 45–65) may have aspired to achieve upward mobility by spending their working years being promoted up the corporate ladder at a single employer, Gen X (aged 30–45) and Gen Y (aged 18–29) members expect to change employers far more frequently.

Higher turnover rates are bad news for sales managers. Experts believe that the total cost of replacing an employee is somewhere around 150 percent of that employee's annual compensation. However, the figure is much higher for sales professionals because their departure may mean the loss of key customers, creating millions of dollars of lost revenue.

Ironically, it's often the coping mechanisms that firms put in place during a downturn that cause sales employees to leave once the economy picks up.

For example, as companies become more concerned with cash flow, sales teams suffer tighter travel budgets, slower payment of expenses and commissions, and less spending on sales training. While these actions may be necessary, they tend to alienate sales professionals, who begin feeling that the firm does not truly support their efforts.

Because of this, sales professionals often emerge from a recession feeling resentment toward their firm and its management. According to the Deloitte survey, almost half of those planning to leave their current job cite a loss of trust in their manager or employer as the primary reason they intended to look for new employment.

This is no secret in the boardroom. Once again, according to the Deloitte survey, fully two-thirds of Fortune 1000 executives understand that a lack of trust and confidence in management can contribute to an increase in job mobility.

In fact, there are probably sales organizations that lose nine out of ten new hires within the first two years, and that figure is just for the average sales professional; fully replacing a top sales professional could easily take longer, if such replacement is even possible. Needless to say, high turnover rates create a constant need for replacement personnel. And that's a big deal when it comes to making sales, because most companies report that it takes six months or longer to ramp up a new sales representative to full productivity.

To make matters worse, the tools that most sales managers have at their disposal are so old and clunky. Sales managers are trying to cope with this roller-coaster of challenges by clinging to sales concepts that are literally decades old. For example, it's possible (easy, in fact) to purchase courses in today's sales training markets that are virtually identical to those presented to the sales teams who were mandated to hawk the Ford Edsel.

While some of that quaint stuff may (possibly) be useful today, it was (and is) entirely based in equal parts upon anecdotes, assumptions, guesswork, and chutzpah, rather than science.

Nowhere is this outmoded thinking more obvious than in the hiring process. There are many executives who believe that they're making a wise hiring decision for a sales job if the candidates are able to make a "good sales pitch" for hiring them. While the ability to present is obviously important, today's sales environments (as described earlier) require far more than a carnival barker's patter.

Many sales managers have also failed in the area of technology. According to a 2001 study by the market research firm the Gartner Group, as many as 50 percent of CRM installations were considered failures—by the people who must use them on a day-to-day basis.

While success rates for CRM are somewhat higher today, failed technology projects inside sales departments are far from unusual, according to CRM consultant Barton Goldenberg of ISMguide.com. "Many companies fail to connect their CRM purchases to the needs of the sales force," he explains. "Sales professionals try, and then reject the system or see it as a nuisance. This ends up wasting money on hardware, software, and training that could be better spent elsewhere."

Sales technology can also cause problems when it bolsters sales behaviors that do not need improvement. For example, a sales professional who is good at presentations but weak in closing is likely to become even less productive when given a tool that improves the quality of his presentations.

That new technology inevitably encourages that professional to continue to focus on presentations, when in fact the real challenge, for that particular sales professional, is setting up the conditions for closing the sale and then asking for the business.

Another area where sales management has struggled is sales training, both internal and external. In the United States alone, companies that sell business-to-business spend between $4 and $7 billion on sales training, according to Dave Stein, CEO of ES Research, a company that studies the sales training market. And yet, much (and even most) of the huge expense is wasted.

The sad truth is that many sales training programs are simply repackaged motivational programs, and even sales training programs that are skills-based run the risk of emphasizing or reinforcing behaviors that are not strategic. For example, suppose an individual sales professional is already a good "closer," but has trouble developing long-term customer relationships. In this case, a course on "how to close" will have only a minimal impact on that person's overall value to the company.

Worst case, it may cause that individual to further neglect elements of the sales process that are required in order to achieve a strategic goal, such as the formation of a stable and loyal customer base.

If there's a failure to correctly diagnose exactly what's not working in the sales process, both at an organizational level and an individual level, sales technology and sales training are only going to make a bad situation worse. Without precise knowledge of exactly where a team or an individual is failing, then throwing technology and training into the mix is a little like a doctor giving a sick patient a random collection of drugs. While a particular drug might work, the patient might get sicker (or even die) due to the side effects.

Sales process is also a source of lost opportunity. In our experience, a surprising number of companies lack even a basic sales process. Instead, they rely upon organizational lore, with individuals passing along "we've always done it this way" information that may encourage sales behaviors that have been creating diminishing returns for years.

Other sales organizations have a sales process in place, but are full of individuals who either don't know how to use it or actively refuse to use it. Unfortunately, many sales managers are reluctant to compel compliance because they're afraid that the process doesn't accurately reflect the best practices of their top performers.

In fact, the top performers are often the worst offenders when it comes to subverting the official process, because the official process, in their experience, doesn't work. Indeed, the process itself is likely to have been constructed based upon untested theories about what "should work" with customers rather than any kind of measurable improvement that can be causally tied to its use.

Still other organizations have a sales process in place and sales professionals who use it religiously, but are still failing because the process does not accurately reflect the strategic needs of the company. For example, a sales process might emphasize prospecting for new business, when the company's business model requires a low cost of sale that's only possible with a high mix of cross-sell and up-sell opportunities.

Sales executives and managers, as a class, are far from unaware of their inability to get a handle on an increasingly complex selling environment. According to *SellingPower* magazine, the typical sales vice president or chief sales officer stays in place for *less than two years*. It would be strange indeed if sales managers facing that kind of pervasive job insecurity didn't realize that sales management is in a more or less permanent state of crisis.

What emerges is a picture of sales management struggling not just with hard economic times, but with economic fluctuations. That failure is characterized by an inability to hire the right people, adequately train the people that they do hire, and a general inability to hold on to those employees who do succeed.

The Advent of Scientific Selling

The solution to the crisis in sales management is to introduce science (and once again, we mean real science, not lip-service science) into sales organizations. With scientific selling, selling (and managing the process) no longer remains a "black art" but becomes more measurable, and more predictable, even in markets that are undergoing massive, rapid change.

Every element of the crisis in sales management emerges from the inability to adequately measure the basic elements that will lead to the creation of a successful sales team.

This is not to say that sales organizations haven't been measuring themselves for years. In fact, there are few corporate organizations that are measured more frequently than sales teams. Unfortunately, when it comes to measurement, most sales organizations focus on downstream measurements such as closes per month, revenue generated, and so forth.

While some organizations also track milestones in the sales process (like conversion rates on cold calling), very few have the tools with which to measure upstream success factors such as the company's ability to hire sales professionals who will work well in that environment. Similarly, most companies lack a way to measure specific sales behaviors such as the ability to develop an initial opportunity, or the ability to present specific benefits to a customer account.

Sales managers who want to build successful sales organizations in an increasingly complex and competitive business environment cannot haphazardly throw technology and training at problems and hope that something sticks. Instead, they take a scientific approach that measures specifically what's needed in each situation. That measurement must then be followed by the specific application of technology and training that addresses specific strengths and weaknesses.

A truly scientific approach demands more. In order to manage a sales organization in today's incredibly demanding business world, sales managers need scientifically valid ways to measure, correct, and improve the building blocks of a successful sales team and sales process. Subsequent chapters in this book describe exactly how that is accomplished, with examples from real life.

Specifically, this book focuses on two scientific disciplines: (1) behavior assessment (which measures the basic psychology, drive, and motivation of the sales employees and managers), and (2) skills assessment (which measures sales employees' specific sales knowledge, skills, and judgment). These two elements correspond roughly to the concept of "nature versus nurture," with behavioral assessment measuring the nature of the individual, and skills assessment measuring the effectiveness of the nurture.

Behavioral assessment provides a way for the sales manager to measure and understand the motivating needs and drives of a firm's top performers and then tune the hiring process to measure for similar traits in future candidates. It also provides insight into the motivational strategies of existing personnel, so that sales management can more easily coach and manage, according to each sales professional's individual needs and personality.

Skills assessment allows a sales manager to extract specific data about the effectiveness of specific sales skills in a sales process, such as building trust and credibility, identifying client needs, presenting products/services, articulating their value, handling objections, gaining agreement for the sale, and finally, creating long-term customer relationships.

Behavioral assessment and skills assessment, when applied in parallel, thus provide sales managers with a perspective into salespeople and the sales process that is simply impossible using the traditional method of "management by gut" and "measuring the results."

Throughout this book, you'll be exposed to some incredible successes that companies have had through the application of science to various aspects of the sales process.

For example, in Chapter 4, you'll learn about Centier Bank, a financial institution with around $2 billion in assets, that used scientific selling to change its hiring practices to increase retention. This solved a major problem, because the company was losing one out of five sales personnel every year and was located in a geographical area where talented sales personnel were particularly difficult to recruit. Using the techniques described in this book, Centier halved that rate to 1 out of 10.

Similarly, in Chapter 6, you'll learn how the information provider LexisNexis used the concepts described in this book to guide their merger and acquisition strategy, and then as a means for making managers better able to coach the individuals who came over with the acquired firms. The result was a turnover rate that shrunk by 50 percent, achieving a final figure that's lower than the industry average, despite all the churn and confusion inherent in corporate mergers.

These are by no means exceptional cases. In fact, the use of the tools described in this book have a consistent and proven positive effect on sales results across the board, according to a recent study by the market research firm the Aberdeen Group. According to their survey, three-quarters of the organizations that used assessments experienced higher management satisfaction in their hiring of sales personnel. These companies also experienced a 75 percent year-over-year decrease in hiring costs and a 2.5 times year-over-year increase in profit for the average sales professional in the organization.

Sales organizations that embrace the concept of selling more scientifically will inevitably become more competitive because they won't be wasting resources focusing on irrelevant or counterproductive activities. They'll have the tools that they need to better assess the performance of candidates and personnel alike, creating a predictable improvement in the organization's ability to deliver sales results. Sales organizations armed with such tools are also more likely to create a sales culture that attracts and keeps personnel who have the basic personality and motivation to be successful in that environment.

2

The Science of Behavioral Assessment

All 70 managers in our organization use PI to better understand how to interact with their team members and how to more effectively coach them on a day-to-day basis. Team members are given their profiles and can share the information with coworkers, if they like. When I looked at my own scores, I was amazed at the level of detail that came out of the results. The information was "bang on" when it came to explain who I was and what drove me.
— Chantal Bedard, Training Manager, Bell Mobility

There are two basic elements to scientific selling: (1) behavior assessment (which measures the basic psychology of the individual), and (2) skills assessment (which measures the individual's sales knowledge, skills, and judgment). These two elements correspond roughly to the concept of "nature versus nurture," with behavioral assessment measuring the nature of the individual, and skills assessment measuring the effectiveness of the nurture. The two measurements demystify the well-known "knowing (skills)—doing (behavior) gap" and provide scientific data to increase performance.

In subsequent chapters, we'll examine how to use these two powerful concepts in parallel in hiring, training, coaching, management, and so forth. However, in order to make those discussions meaningful, it's first necessary to explain some basic concepts and some of the science behind the concepts. This chapter does that for behavioral assessment, while the next chapter covers skills assessment.

Behavioral Assessment

Every sales manager (and indeed every manager) faces the following questions on a day-to-day basis:

* Who do I hire?
* Who do I promote?
* Who is my next leader?
* How do I keep my people engaged?
* How do I motivate my people?
* How do I bring together my team?
* How are my people going to react to change?
* How do I impact performance daily?
* How does my management style impact my people?

All of these issues are obviously crucial to addressing the challenges that sales managers face every day. Because of this, it's worthwhile to take a close look at behavioral science and behavioral assessment, and how it's being used in business today.

Traditionally, sales managers have addressed these questions on an ad-hoc basis, using a combination of gut feeling and trial-and-error. The results have been haphazard at best. Fortunately, there is a different, scientifically proven way to address these challenges: behavioral assessment.

Behavioral assessment is the practical branch of behavioral science, a field that looks at individuals and their behavior along with their interaction with groups, cultures, and processes. Rooted in foundational research beginning almost 100 years ago, behavioral science provides empirical data with broad applications to business. The most fundamental of the applications is the tremendous amount of insight into a person's behavior allowing organizations to make better decisions.

As workplace complexity grows and jobs become more complex, more technological, and more specialized, the measurement of personality is becoming an increasingly important part of matching individuals to the job roles for which they are best suited. Behavioral assessment helps to answer the litany of decisions needed to drive sales results.

Behavioral scientists have done extensive research into motivation and human behavior and have formulated behavioral models based on their research. While much of that research is highly technical, there are some general observations about which most scientists working in the field agree:

- Our behavior is governed by two types of interactions: those that come naturally (instincts) and those that are learned (conditioning).
- Conditioning begins early in our lives and drives major changes in subsequent behavior based upon the variety and quality of our experiences.
- All things being equal, a particular individual will behave in the same way today that he/she did yesterday and will behave in the same way tomorrow.
- No individual does anything until and unless he or she is first motivated. However, each of us can be motivated only by our own felt or perceived needs.
- Your perceptions of need cannot motivate me, and my perceptions cannot motivate you. Only your needs motivate you, and only my needs motivate me.

These observations provide a scientific basis for the perhaps intuitive truth that leaders can never assume that anybody is motivated by the same needs that motivate us or anyone else.

Behavioral science has also identified common themes that drive human motivation. These include:

- *Goals*: Humans are goal-oriented creatures, so when goals are set, they tend to drive behavior.
- *Pleasure/Pain*: Humans prefer pleasure to pain and will seek positive outcomes and states and avoid negative ones.
- *Mastery and Control*: Humans prefer mastery and control to ambiguity and uncertainty and these factors directly impact their confidence and efficiency.
- *Variety and Interest*: Humans generally prefer interesting, stimulating, and satisfying to boring, stressful, and repetitious activities.
- *Social Context*: Humans are social creatures and are constantly involved in a series of social interactions and social comparisons. They want to both get ahead and get along.
- *Genetics*: Humans are all unique with genetic and personal backgrounds that shape our wants, desires, and reactions to events.

Although these concepts/drives exist in all people, the amount and degree that each one motivates a person varies widely. One person may be highly motivated by variety while another is more comfortable with things being steady and even. The first person may be better suited to outside sales in a position that requires them to meet new people all the time, while the second person is likely to be better suited to an account management position where they service the same customers over time.

This is a most important point. Sales managers use behavioral assessments because they are an accurate predictor of human behavior—giving insight into how a person will be over the long haul. Because of that, they help sales managers cope with the challenges of hiring, retaining, motivating, and developing top sales talent.

Behavioral Surveys

A key concept in behavioral assessment is the behavioral survey, which is a way to specifically examine the psychological profile of an individual or a group of individuals.

This application of behavioral assessment techniques in business situations is based on certain fundamental assumptions of behavioral psychology, such that work and social behavior are primarily an expression in activity of a variety of responses to environmental stimuli, recognizable as consistently expressed personality traits. Because behavior is both consistent and predictable, behavioral surveys provide powerful data in the understanding of people at work.

Behavioral surveys provide a measurable way to compare the performance of different types of people inside different jobs. For example, one of the proverbial failings of people who start their own companies is that, as the company grows, it outgrows their ability to manage. While there are highly visible counterexamples (like Microsoft's Bill Gates and Facebook's Mark Zuckerberg), most startups eventually go through some sort of management change when the company grows beyond the startup phase. Why is this?

The use of a behavioral survey can provide an answer. For example, PI Europe, a member firm of PI Worldwide, recently helped to sponsor a survey of 227 finalists for the Ireland Ernst and Young Entrepreneur of the Year program over the last 12 years. The purpose of this quantitative psychological test was to determine the psychological factors that drive a person to act in an entrepreneurial manner.

The study revealed that 82 percent of the entrepreneurs studied were assertive, self-confident, challenging, venturesome, independent, and competitive individuals, while 85 percent had low patience and tended to be tense, restless, and driving individuals, who work with a profound sense of urgency.

From this, it was concluded that successful entrepreneurs and innovators approach life with a hypothesis-testing mind-set, and seek to cultivate that mind-set in others, and tend to be more independent in putting forth their own ideas, respond well to pressure and challenge, and will resourcefully work through and around roadblocks to achieve their goals.

However, while that's a useful profile for somebody starting a company, it describes a set of characteristics that are not as applicable to a traditional management role, according to Steve Waterhouse, president of Predictive Results, a PI Worldwide member firm that uses behavior surveys to study employee behavior. "A great manager has to have empathy," he explains. "It's not a manager's job to make herself successful. It's to make her staff successful."

This is not to say that it's impossible for an entrepreneur to become an effective manager in a more traditional environment. However, there is definitely a measurable difference in the behavioral profiles of the most successful entrepreneurs and the most successful large company executive managers.

A similar dynamic plays itself out inside sales organizations. It's not uncommon for a company to promote a top sales professional to a management job, in the mistaken belief that the behavior and skills will map well from the old to the new job. However, that is not always (or even often) the case. Many times, the newly promoted sales manager cannot resist closing the deal rather than coaching his or her employee to do so.

As a result, companies that use behavioral surveys to better understand the motivation and skills of their employees tend to offer additional career paths and incentives than simply promotion to a management job. Behavioral assessment helps a manager "figure out what motivates an employee and treat each one as if they are special and unique," says Waterhouse.

Business Applications of Behavioral Science

Forward-looking companies are using behavioral assessment in the following ways:

- *Hiring Decisions.* The foundation of a successful hire is a strong job fit—finding the best fit between a person's natural ability to do the job, the requirements of the job, and the culture of the organization. Other key components of the selection process include performance criteria and specific experience, education, and skills. Sales performance criteria may include past sales experience, closing rate, and type of sales. Behavioral assessment can also be used to write an effective ad to attract candidates, to design key interview questions based on fit/gap between the profile of the job and the profile of the candidate, and to analyze the job fit between various candidates and the position.

- *Employee Motivation.* The need to motivate and engage employees is foundational for managers in order to grow teams and create substantial business results. Behavioral assessment provides the data necessary for managers to recognize and understand the person's motivating needs. Once a person's needs are met, employees attain a high level of achievement, increase productivity, are motivated and engaged. Motivated and engaged people are achievers and often realize higher than expected levels of success. Having a deep understanding of what motivates the sales reps allows the manager to provide sales management interventions like training, coaching, and mentoring with laser accuracy.

- *Job Feedback*. Everyone working in every business organization needs some feedback from the work environment and the people who are responsible for it. The reasons for that need differ with different individuals, but the need is universal. Individual needs for communication on a personal level range from the need for assurance of security to the need for assurance of recognition or opportunity. Insufficient communication causes uncertainty, which causes low morale and a negative attitude; this is particularly true during periods of change. Management's attention to the quality, style, and frequency of communications is critical to employee satisfaction. There may be a difference between the sales manager's need for communication and the sales rep's, and understanding and bridging that gap is the job of the sales manager.

- *Managing Conflict*. Working with others inevitably includes conflict. Behavioral assessment can provide objective information about the root of the conflict and provides a nonthreatening way to discuss difficult situations. By bridging the conflict with data, both parties feel respected, listened to, and can work together to resolve outstanding issues. This allows managers to focus on the human analytics behind the conflict rather than to focus solely on the issue at hand. Working to resolve the root cause creates a long-term solution to the conflict. This information can be applied to all situations, such as the relationship between the manager and the rep, the rep and other reps, and the rep and others within the organization.

- *Team Building*. Effective teams, whether departmental, across functions, or at the board of directors level, pride themselves on superior communication, decision making, productivity, and morale. Understanding how people work together is the key. Behavioral assessment helps to provide objective information about the motivational needs and work behaviors of individual group members that helps to bridge gaps, maximize the strengths of each team member, and ultimately apply these strengths to achieve common goals. Pairing inside and outside sales reps or creating a high performance sales team takes superior team-building skills by the manager; data eliminates guesswork and provides concrete data on the individuals and the team dynamics.

- *Performance Management*. Performance management is often about helping an employee to do more or less of a particular aspect of their role, to fill in gaps, and to improve overall performance. Behavioral assessment provides insight into the motivation and drive of current behaviors as well as providing information to help the employee embrace a change. Equipped with real data, the manager increases their ability to impact change and long-term performance management. Whether delivering tough feedback or inspiring the rep to do more, the insight from behavioral assessments allows the manager to form the message in a way that is best received by the rep.

- *Coaching*. One-on-one coaching is an important way to help executive team members develop leadership skills to build stronger relationships with each other, and to more skillfully develop their direct reports. Behavioral assessment provides key insights into a person's natural behavior and workplace drives. It provides managers with insight about their own behavioral needs and coaching style as well as information about the person they are coaching. Armed with concrete data, a manager's coaching time increases in efficiency and effectiveness—understanding exactly what their people need to increase their performance and how to best have coaching conversations. Tailoring the coaching to the needs of the rep gives the manager the ability to impact change faster and for the long term.

- *Structural Changes.* Often, large organizations undergoing change initiatives such as mergers and acquisitions and restructuring of a sales team typically require many of these applications. In these circumstances, behavioral assessment serves as a foundational tool across the organization for data-based decision making. Through the use of behavioral assessment, organizations are provided with insight into current, or potential, leaders' natural behaviors and styles and how they engage with others, as well as assessing their role in team leadership dynamics.

- *Employee Retention.* Although many organizations focus on getting the right people on board, talent retention is a top priority for the entire life cycle of the employee. Successful organizations realize that an effective employee retention strategy provides the foundation for sustainable growth and superior performance. Those that fail to make employee retention a priority are at risk of losing their top talent to the competition. In addition, increasing retention drastically reduces the high cost of turnover, eliminating not only out-of-pocket expenses related to recruitment, selection, and severance, but also in lost opportunity, productivity, and morale. Behavioral assessment provides managers with data to increase employee retention by meeting the needs of their people.

- *Succession Planning.* Needless to say, this is an important component of preparing a company for the future. Behavioral assessment combined with other data points such as experience, education, interests, and successes provides outstanding information to identify future leaders and to build a solid plan to bring a company forward. Depending on the phase of the company from start-up to mature, the needs of the company and its leadership may evolve; behavioral assessment helps put the right team into place.

The Effectiveness of Behavioral Assessment

Behavioral assessment is measurably effective in the performance of employees; according to a recent study, Assessments 2011: Selecting and Developing for the Future, by research and market intelligence firm Aberdeen Group of over 640 organizations including 516 currently using assessments as part of their talent strategy. Within that survey base, Aberdeen looked for firms it characterized as "Best-in-Class," based upon the following three key performance criteria:

1. Seventy-three percent of employees received a rating of "exceeds expectations" on last performance review.
2. Sixty-nine percent of key positions have at least one willing and able successor identified.
3. There was a 19 percent year-over-year improvement in hiring manager satisfaction.

Aberdeen discovered that those firms that fell into this best-in-class category shared several common characteristics, including:

- The use of assessments as a tool to drive better talent decisions at multiple points in the employee life cycle, from hiring to succession
- Collaboration between HR and the business to create a language of competencies to assess against
- Use of a variety of assessment types, appropriate to the decision point, to help them minimize the risk in critical talent decisions
- Use of assessment data to help identify talent gaps and available talent resources to support long-term workforce and business planning
- Assess not only for current skills, but also for future leadership and development potential

The common theme differentiating best-in-class organizations in the use of assessments was the maturity they demonstrated in trusting the data as a key voice in the talent decision-making process. Across the board, at every decision point, best-in-class companies placed greater value on assessment data as a part of that decision process.

Significantly, the decision point where there was the greatest gap between best-in-class firms and the other firms was in helping to understand future potential. Aberdeen felt that this was particularly important because it indicates that these top performing companies know that it's not enough just to understand an employee's current capabilities, but what they may be able to do in the future. It also indicates that these organizations acknowledge that gut instinct alone is not enough to help them make the call on evaluating future potential.

The Aberdeen research concluded that "as every business decision falls under greater scrutiny, organizations are looking for tools that help them make better choices.... Assessments can provide valuable insights into hiring, promotion and development decisions, and help organizations minimize talent risk while maximizing talent performance."[1]

How to Choose a Behavioral Assessment Method

An Internet search for "behavioral assessments" typically generates links to between two hundred and three hundred different assessments available in the marketplace. However, not all assessments are equal. To be appropriate for business use, the assessments must possess the following four characteristics:

1. *Reliability*. This refers to the consistency and stability of a measurement instrument. If the concept being measured is consistent, such as a personality trait, then the measurement instrument should yield similar results if the same person responds to it a number of times.

---

[1] www.aberdeen.com/aberdeen-library/6996/RA-talent-performance-assessment.aspx.

2. *Validity.* This refers to the accuracy of the measurement instrument. A measurement instrument is valid if it actually measures what it purports to measure. Construct validity is demonstrated when a measurement instrument is statistically compared with another measure of similar and/or different concepts that has been soundly constructed and is generally accepted. In essence, the tool has to be able to prove what it says it's measuring with empirical data.

3. *No Adverse Impact.* This means that the instrument has been studied and statistically evaluated to ensure it is free from bias and that some sample populations do not demonstrate an advantage in scoring based on the instrument. An instrument is considered to have no adverse impact when no sample populations (such as gender groups, age groups, or racial groups) are statistically disadvantaged in measurement by the instrument. As you can imagine, adverse impact would carry significant legal ramifications in business.

4. *Compliance.* Compliance with government regulations is also important to consider when using a behavioral instrument. Governmental bodies, such as the U.S. Equal Employment Opportunity Commission and similar organizations around the world, set forth guidelines for the proper use of practices (such as the use of behavioral instruments) in hiring and other personnel matters. Using any type of instrument that does not follow the standards of your governing body should be avoided in business.

Of the numerous behavioral assessment methodologies that are in wide use today, there are many that fulfill these four criteria. They include Caliper, Hogan, Kenexa, DDI, 16PF (published by IPAT), and SHL (which is popular internationally).

Due to the author's familiarity with the Predictive Index (PI), this behavioral methodology will be used throughout this book for examples and case studies. However, it must be emphasized that other, scientifically valid, behavioral survey methodologies (including those previously mentioned) can, and are, used for scientific sales management.

The PI is one of a class of objective assessment techniques based on certain fundamental assumptions of behavioral psychology—the first being that work/social behavior is primarily an expression in activity of a variety of responses to environmental stimuli, recognizable as consistently expressed personality traits.

The PI was developed and administered experimentally by Arnold S. Daniels during the early 1950s, when it was soon made available for industrial use. It takes the form of a checklist of words and phrases that stimulate a reaction in the person being measured. Confronted with the stimuli in the survey, the individual will respond to them, either positively or negatively, in a manner consistent with the ways in which he/she responds to the actual environmental stimuli that the words in the checklist symbolize.

The PI measures seven drives and motivations:
1. The drive to influence people and events
2. The drive for social interaction
3. The intensity of a person's tension and pace
4. The drive to conform to formal rules
5. The individual's approach to decision making
6. The individual's response to stimulus that impacts their stamina and ability
7. The individual's morale

This data provides insight on how the individual will approach elements of the business environment such as leadership, communication, risk-taking, leading change, and decision making. In addition to measuring actual behavior in the work environment, the Predictive Index also provides unique measurements of the effect of that environment on the individual.

In the PI system, a key role is played by the PI analyst who can help a manager to understand the PI, interpret the data, and use the PI in everyday business decisions. A PI analyst is an individual who has received in-depth training in the use of the Predictive Index System through the PI Management Workshop. Senior leaders, managers at all levels, talent management professionals, human resources partners, and key individual contributors are all candidates to become PI analysts within an organization.

Trained PI analysts with management responsibilities use the PI to manage their own people. The PI analysts in support functions provide insight for managers' decision making in "people" situations. The PI analysts also help to identify and develop high potential talent and provide the foundation for leadership development. Trained PI analysts can also manage and provide insight for other managers, and can help identify and develop new talent with those organizations.

TIME LINE: Behavior Science and Management

* *1913: John B. Watson* publishes what's known as "The Behaviorist Manifesto." In the article, Watson outlined the major features of his new philosophy, which is that psychology, rather than something mysterious, should be a purely objective experimental branch of natural science. Its theoretical goal is the prediction and control of behavior.

* *1921: Hermann Rorschach* in the book *Psychodiagnostics* explains how to scientifically analyze the data from information gathered experimentally. While his basic inkblot test is not particularly applicable to businesses, his concept of using scientific algorithms to analyze psychological data is a mainstay of behavior science.

* *1934: Louis L. Thurstone* publishes an article, "The Vectors of the Mind," describing his discovery that various

people will respond positively to certain descriptive words by checking them, and negatively to others by not checking them. He developed what he called "clusters" of words to which persons with certain predominant personality traits will consistently respond.

• *1943: Abraham Maslow* begins work on his "Hierarchy of Needs," a pyramid depicting the levels of human needs, psychological and physical. At the bottom of the pyramid are basic needs like food and water and sex, followed by safety needs like security and order. The next level consists of the psychological needs of love and belonging, while the fourth level is concerned with achieving success and status. The top of the pyramid is self-actualization, which occurs when individuals reach a state of harmony and understanding.

• *1953: Arnold S. Daniels* develops and administers experimentally the Predictive Index (PI). It was made available for industrial use, and the Predictive Index Management Training Course was first conducted for a management group by Mr. Daniels in July 1955. Since then, the PI Management Workshop, which is currently available in 60 languages plus braille, has been administered millions of times.

• *1959: Frederick Herzberg* proposes the "Two-Factor Theory," that people are influenced by two sets of factors: (1) Motivation (achievement, recognition, work itself, responsibility, promotion, and growth), and (2) Hygiene (pay/benefits, company policy/administration, relationships with coworkers, supervision, status, job security, working conditions, and personal life). He discovers, among other things, that the prevention of dissatisfaction is just as important as encouragement.

• *1964: Victor Vroom* conceives "Expectancy Theory," which proposes that a person will decide to behave or act in a certain way because they are motivated to select a specific behavior over other behaviors due to what they expect the result of that selected behavior will be. The theory emphasizes the need for organizations to relate rewards directly to performance and to ensure that the rewards provided are those rewards deserved and wanted by the recipients.

- *1975: Richard Hackman and Greg Oldham* propose the "Job Characteristics Model," which studies how particular job characteristics impact on job outcomes, including job satisfaction. The model states that there are five core job characteristics (skill variety, task identity, task significance, autonomy, and feedback) that impact three critical psychological states (experienced meaningfulness, experienced responsibility for outcomes, and knowledge of the actual results), in turn influencing work outcomes (job satisfaction, absenteeism, work motivation, etc.).

- *1990: Edwin Locke and Gary Latham* publish *A Theory of Goal Setting and Task Performance*, which defines goal setting as establishing specific, measurable, and time-targeted objectives. They discover that goals perceived as realistic are more effective in changing behavior, and that setting goals is a process that allows people to specify and then work toward their own objectives, most commonly with financial or career-based goals.

- *2006: Richard Arvey* uses studies of identical twins to investigate the genetic influences of work behavior, such as job satisfaction and leadership. His studies found that approximately 40 percent of the variance in leadership is genetically influenced while environmental factors contribute to the remaining differences.

In the next chapter, we'll discuss the other side of the scientific selling equation: skills assessment.

3

The Science of Sales Skills Assessment

We use these tools both proactively and reactively. I use them for manpower planning in all our branches so that I'm sure we have the right number of task-oriented individuals versus people-oriented. We've been driving hard to get more socially oriented people to build better relationships and develop opportunities for referrals and cross-sales.
> —Clayton Mersereau, SVP of Branch Administration, Enterprise Bank

I n the previous chapter, we learned about behavioral assessment, a scientific methodology for measuring the basic psychology, drive, and motivation of the individual. In this chapter, we'll be discussing skills assessment, which is measuring the individual's sales skills, knowledge, and judgment. Specifically, we'll be discussing skills assessment when it comes to specific sales skills required of individuals who sell.

Skills assessment adds a critical dimension to behavioral assessment, because it measures something that can be changed. Behavioral assessment primarily measures characteristics that are part of a person's basic personality. As such, they assess the potential of an individual to be successful at a given job or sales position.

By contrast, skills assessment measures the depth of sales knowledge needed in actual sales situations, in the specific activities and actions that the sales professional takes. Two individuals with very similar PI measurements (i.e., who score similarly in behavioral assessment) can have wildly different skill assessment measurements, as the result of prior training, business experience, and so forth.

However, unlike behavioral assessment, which was a practical application of behavioral science, sales skill assessment has a somewhat colorful background that's played itself out in the context of popular culture over the past 100 years. As a result, it's only been quite recently—within the past two decades—that it's become a truly scientific discipline.

The History of Sales Skill Assessment

Attempts to measure sales skills are nothing new. At the first World Salesmanship Conference in 1916, two professors from the Carnegie Institute of Technology publicly performed mental alertness tests upon 25 young men, in order to determine which of them would be most likely to succeed in the sales profession.

The results of that early test appear to be lost. That's probably no great loss, however, since the science included in the conference was not by any means up to modern standards. For example, the conference featured a lecture by a well-known practitioner of phrenology, pseudoscience primarily focused on measurements of the human skull. This speaker (who was evidently taken quite seriously) explained that the best sales professionals always have a "high forehead" and counseled sales managers to specifically avoid candidates with "a flat back head."

As bizarre as that advice sounds today, it is representative of a major theme in skills assessment: the intrusion of various kinds of intuitive truths posing as scientific data. For decades, sales gurus of all types have positioned their concepts as scientific when in fact they are not scientific at all, but rather attempts to borrow credibility by claiming to be scientific.

For example, a glance through the large lexicon of sales books finds several that claim to be scientific but, when examined, turn out to be filled with the usual combination of anecdotes and homilies. Very little, if any, measurement is attempted, and then only of the most general kind (e.g., "after we trained them, they doubled their sales").

Pseudoscientific interpretations of sales activities have been common because academia (where most groundbreaking science is performed) has only recently become interested in selling as a human behavior. Even today, less than 50 business schools (out of several thousand worldwide) offer courses in selling, and there are very few psychologists who have interested themselves in the subject.

There are several reasons for this. First, conventional wisdom is that sales professionals don't need anything other than a high school diploma (if that) in order to sell. While they might need some technical training to sell a particular product, and may need to learn some sales skills, what's important (according to this theory) is that they have the right personality. As we saw in the previous chapter, that's true to a certain extent (although today some sales positions require extensive training).

Because there was no apparent reason to offer college degrees in selling, academics have traditionally shied away from it, preferring instead to focus on marketing, which seems more professional. What developed, over the years, was a bias inside academia against the sales profession. For example, Peter Drucker, perhaps the most influential academic in the field of business and management, famously expressed the opinions that the aim of marketing is to make selling superfluous.

What little analysis was applied to the activities of selling focused on reducing them to highly ritualized behaviors that any sufficiently motivated individual could execute. Sales training courses in the 1930s and 1940s, for example, described such minutiae as exactly how to hand the pen to the customer when asking them to sign the contract. The only measurement that took place was whether the customer bought or failed to buy. The behaviors themselves were not considered worthy of measurement, in any academic sense.

The Advent of Sales Process

This overly simplistic approach to selling began to change in the 1970s, due primarily to change in the type of products being sold, particularly in the business-to-business (B2B) environment. Previously, salespeople (in both business and consumer environments) were seen primarily as carriers of information and order writers.

In the 1970s, however, computers began changing how businesses operate. These changes, and the technology required to make them happen, required expertise that lay far beyond the world of the sales pitch and the handy fountain pen. Customers wanted and needed solutions, so it's not surprising that a new model of selling emerged from the world of office automation.

This concept, called "solution selling," emerged simultaneously inside IBM, Wang Laboratories, Xerox, and a number of other high-tech firms of the period. While the old concept of selling emphasized ritualized behavior, solution selling had the salesperson focus on the customer's needs (specifically problems that create pain) and addresses the issue with customized offerings.

A solution selling concept assumed a sales process (or cycle) that consisted of several (or all) of the following steps:

1. Prospect for new customers
2. Diagnose customer needs

3. Craft a potential solution
4. Establish value
5. Bargain for access to decision makers
6. Position proof, return on investment (ROI), and the total solution
7. Negotiate a win-win
8. Following up to ensure customer success

This solution selling concept rapidly disseminated to other industries as they changed their business model and structure to take advantage of computer technology. Most companies today, for instance, have complicated supply chains where they would, in the past, have had their own vertical structures to create component parts, or distribute goods. Each element of a complex supply chain represents a solution sell where the sales professional is taking over a key element of the customer's business, adapting his or her offering to the specific needs of that customer.

Unfortunately, solution selling was never able to fully shed the concept of ritualized behaviors. Often it depended upon sales prompters and sales scripts, which were supposed to guide conversations but, when executed, simply irritated prospects and customers. More importantly, the effectiveness was seldom, if ever, measured. Instead it was assumed, even though there was no statistical way to look at its impact. And when solution selling failed to produce results, that failure was always attributed to the unwillingness or inability of the individual sales rep to execute the techniques.

The Limitations of Sales Process

It wasn't until sales process was itself codified into computer systems that any form of measurement took place. The first commercial attempts to use computers to track sales activity was in the 1980s. These systems were known collectively as Sales Force Automation (SFA), a terminology that clearly reveals the bias toward viewing selling as a ritualized activity comparable to working on an assembly line.

The emphasis of SFA (and its later successor, Computer Relationship Management or CRM) was to make the sales process of solution selling more repeatable and standardized. Sales professionals were expected and encouraged to follow a standard set of behaviors at each stage of the process. They would then log the results of their activities, much like a factory automation system monitors the steps in a manufacturing line.

Because such systems generally force sales reps to do a lot of keystroking on top of their normal duties, they have not proven very popular among sales professionals. In addition, the factory model of sales automation tended to ignore the rather obvious fact that customers might have a very different idea of how they would like the buying processes to proceed.

Nevertheless, the storing of data into a database allowed sales managers to examine quantitative data like the conversion rate of leads to prospects to customers. Suddenly sales was measurable in a way that had never been possible in the past. It was now possible to use computers to document what happened and therefore (theoretically at least) to replicate successful sales situations and diagnose (and avoid) those that failed.

Unfortunately, the solution selling model, with its dependence upon a factory model of sales process tended to ignore the fact that customers might have a very different idea of how they would like the buying processes to proceed. The entire basis of solution selling still assumed that selling was a simple, repeatable process that was the same for each individual, regardless of that person's basic personality and skill set.

More importantly, while SFA and CRM did allow the statistical measurement of conversion rates, what was being measured was purely the results of sales activities, not those activities themselves. As such, such measurement could only provide the most basic and gross level of understanding of what was actually going on during actual sales situations involving individual sellers and buyers.

This limitation was most obvious when the statistical measurement of sales process steps was taken before and after sales training. For example, training on cold calling techniques might result in a higher overall conversion rate of leads into prospects. It might even reveal specific improvements in conversion rates for one sales professional as opposed to another.

However, none of that measurement could reveal the "why" behind the improvement (or lack of it). This was partly because of the backward-looking method of measurement. But the limitation was also a natural result of treating sales activity as a set of ritualized activities, executed in a particular order. Something more was needed.

Evolution of Sales Skills

Over time, the limitations of sales process (both in terms of measurement and in terms of having a positive impact on sales) have become clear to sales managers and sales professionals, as well as the people who train them. As a result, there's been a gradual shift in thinking about what's important in sales situations.

While this shift has taken many forms, it generally consists of a shift away from the combination of ritualized behaviors and sales milestones and shifts toward examining, understanding, and reinforcing the general skills that come to play during sales situations. There are many examples of this new kind of thinking in the sales training marketplace including: *Customer-Centric Selling* (Bosworth), *The New Solution Selling* (Eades), and so forth.

For the purposes of this book, the key rethinking of sales process is the methodology known as Customer-Focused Selling (CFS). The reason that CFS is important to the science of sales skills is that, while CFS bears a resemblance to other sales skill models, it is one of the few that can be measured scientifically. A complete description of CFS and how it related to the SSAT is provided in Chapter 8 of this book.

We'll be learning about the measurement methodology later in this chapter. However, for that discussion to make sense, it's first necessary to summarize the CFS methodology and understand how it (and methodologies like it) are different from the ritualized sales skills model that were popular in the past.

Customer-Focused Selling has two key characteristics that make it unique from the classic ritualized sales models of the past. The first is that it comes from the point of view of the customer—instead of "me about me" selling, it is all about "me in reference to you." The strong focus on the buyer's world rather than the seller's is translated in each skill related to the sales process.

The second area that is different is reliance on the sophistication of judgment of the sales rep. Gone are the rote methodologies of a memorized opening, a rigid way to close the sale, or presenting according to a prescribed plan. The emphasis is on being able to understand a situation rapidly and apply judgment of how to utilize that information in each step of the sales process, synthesize the information in front of them, their products and services, and manage the sales process accordingly.

The CFS approach to selling is built on the premise that process drives sales and that skills drive process. That equation helps to link process and skills correctly. Process is the road map that helps the rep advance the sale. Skills are the steps inside that provide the knowledge to execute flawlessly.

Limitations of Solution Selling

The older, ritualized models of selling used a "he says that . . . you say this . . ." approach. For example, Bosworth's original solution selling model was to create a series of sales prompters, lists of relevant questions prepared especially for each type of decision maker within the customer organization. These were categorized into two types:

1. *Diagnostic Questions.* These help customers articulate needs and goals by identifying potential problems and potential opportunities that are biased to the seller's capabilities.
2. *Usage Scenario Questions.* These help customers visualize how their problems can be solved and their goals achieved through the use of your product.

Under this model, the salesperson asks the diagnostic questions first and then, based upon the responses, asks the appropriate usage scenario questions. For example, if a salesperson were selling an inventory control system to a manufacturing firm, he or she might use the following diagnostic questions:

1. How often are products late because component parts aren't in the supply chain?
2. How do you deal with customers whose products aren't shipped on time?
3. Have you ever lost orders or even customers because products weren't shipped on time?

Assuming that the first set of questions exposed a customer need, the salesperson would move to a related set of usage scenario questions, such as:

1. Would it have a positive financial impact on your company if there were one-tenth as many inventory failures as you currently experience?
2. When you have a delay in shipments, would it be useful to be able to automatically inform all your customers that their shipment will be late?

3. When dates for delivery of components slip, would you like the system to identify all orders that will be impacted so that you can proactively notify customers and minimize the impact to your business?

It was assumed that customers would be willing to participate in this ritualized interchange, even though (as many sales professionals can attest) customers often have their own idea of where they'd like a sales conversation to go.

The CFS approach assumes that, rather than a ritualized interchange, there will be conversation during which the sales professional will be able to introduce questions that encourage the customer to expound on their problems, goals, and so forth. There's no assumption of a scripted interchange; instead, the skill lies in being able to listen and adapt to what the customer is saying.

The Selling Skills Assessment Tool (SSAT)

The most significant way that CFS is different from other sales skills methodologies is that it not only can be measured scientifically, but has connected with it a scientifically proven measurement vehicle. In 1999, the author of this book developed the Selling Skills Assessment Tool (SSAT), a scenario-based measurement instrument that examines five specific skill areas that surround the sales/influence skills competency.

The SSAT is a diagnostic instrument specifically designed to quantify the sales and judgment skills of each member of the sales team and to help sales managers identify gaps between sales skills, behavior, and results. The SSAT contains 25 targeted questions to assess the critical selling skills in the CFS model as defined earlier.

The results of the SSAT provide an objective view of sales strengths, skills, and areas that warrant improvement. They provide a statistical evaluation of each of these five core sales skills for their sales force and compare each salesperson to the division/team and to the entire sales force. The SSAT information also provides sales management with specific quantitative data profiling the targeted needs of the group, the needs of the division/team, and the needs of each individual salesperson.

For example, a client company may learn from the SSAT that the entire organization needs training in listening skills. They may learn that one group needs specific training in questioning skills. They may also learn that there is great skill knowledge diversity among participants and that this need is best served by individual coaching rather than group training. The targeted information from the SSAT measurement helps the organization to provide specific training and coaching for the development of their people.

More advanced organizations use the SSAT as part of their Level 5 measurement system to determine the ROI of training initiatives. The SSAT is administered as the benchmark measurement within Level 3 to define the behaviors that must change as the knowledge and skills are applied in the work setting. The SSAT is often then administered 6–12 months later against Level 4 measurements (what they are seeing for results in the organization) and in Level 5 to determine the return on their training investment.

The SSAT can work as a stand-alone diagnostic or as part of a more rigorous Level 5 measurement system within an organization. In all cases, the objective of the SSAT is to provide both the management team and the participant an opportunity to assess individual and group skill level and measure the overall effectiveness of training initiatives.

It is important to emphasize that the scientific validity of the SSAT has been proven numerous times. The SSAT has been administered to business clients ranging from executives, sales reps, managers, and front line staff, across all industries. To date the SSAT has been administered to over 20,000 individuals in North America, Europe, and Asia. The SSAT now has 24 different job and/or industry-specific versions (i.e.,

Outside Sales, Call Center, Health care, Banking, etc.) and is currently available in English, Spanish, German, French, Danish, Dutch, Italian, Swedish, Romanian, Hungarian, Russian, Mandarin Chinese, Korean, and Japanese.

Multiple studies completed on the SSAT have proven reliability (freedom from bias) across all Equal Employment Opportunity Commission (EEOC) required fields including ethnicity, age, and sex. There are studies currently being conducted on the SSAT to prove validity in additional business applications.

In 2005, the author of this book conducted an independent research project in partial fulfillment of the requirements for the degree of Master of Education in Psychological Studies at Cambridge College in Massachusetts. In that study, the author used the field of psychological counseling to test whether the soft skills measurement in the SSAT could be applied outside of sales situations.

In subsequent chapters, we'll examine how both behavioral assessment and skills assessment can be used in a variety of tactical sales and sales management scenarios. In the next chapter, we'll examine specifically how behavioral assessment can be used to make better hiring decisions.

TIME LINE: History of Skills Assessment

- *1904: P.W. Searles* publishes an article in *System* magazine describing how companies were beginning to implement sales processes. The thrust of these programs was to make sales more uniform, predictable, and (most importantly) reproducible. Sales reps were told specific ways to stand, specific words to say, and even specific gestures to make while selling.
- *1916: D.M. Barret*, publisher of *Salesmanship* magazine hosts the first sales training conference, attended by executives from Ford Motor Company, Equitable Life Assurance, Burroughs Adding Machine, and National

Cash Register. A group of 25 young men are given mental alertness tests in an early attempt to quantify their ability to sell, while a phrenologist recommends hiring sales reps who have high foreheads.

- *1926: A.J. Snow* publishes *Psychology of Personal Selling*, an early attempt to explain selling and buying as a form of neuroscience. While he lacked equipment for precise measurement, he speculated upon the behavior of nerve cells in the brain and other physiological changes that take place during decision making.
- *1933: Charles Bennet* publishes *Scientific Salesmanship*, which explained selling behavior in the context of overall economic activity and growth. Like other experts of the period, he sees salesmanship primarily as a form of applied enthusiasm, channeled through a specific set of exterior, highly ritualized selling behaviors.
- *1950s: Ron Popeil* begins pitching consumer products on television, using the highly ritualized selling techniques pioneered in earlier decades. Over time, the concept of a sales pitch becomes a well-defined part of popular culture, making traditional selling techniques seem increasingly artificial and ineffective.
- *1968: Og Mandino* publishes *The Greatest Salesman in the World*. This story of a poor camel boy who achieves a life of abundance becomes wildly popular, reinforcing the notion that learning to sell is primarily a matter of mastering simple skills. He lays out a 10-month program of repetitive readings intended to generate self-improvement.
- *1975: Frank Watts* develops the sales process known as solution selling, which is later popularized by Mike Bosworth and Keith Eades, and scores of imitators. It propounds a series of rote questions intended to help sales professionals prospect, diagnose needs, craft a solution, and so forth. No attempt is made to measure effectiveness.

- *1999: Nancy Martini* (formerly Stephens) creates the SSAT, a scenario-based measurement instrument that examines 25 aspects of selling clustered into five specific skill areas that surround the sales/influence skills competency, tying it to the successful Customer-Focused Selling (CFS) methodology.

4

The Science of Hiring Sales Talent

In the past, I had an idea of the kind of person I wanted to hire. I'd even write out a list of 10 or 20 adjectives describing what I thought a hardened salesperson should be like. Even so, it was all touchy-feely and subjective. Now I have a PRO, and do a PI for every serious job candidate. It's not the be-all and end-all; you still have to take into account the SSAT, age, experience, and the interview. Even so, I rarely interview anyone who is outside the PRO, because it describes the behavior I'm looking for.

— Harley Ostlund, President, Harden Manufacturing

P robably the most important task in every sales manager's job description is hiring the right people. Unfortunately, most sales managers have only the vaguest idea of how to go about doing this.

Sales managers understand they need candidates who can be a trusted advisor to their customers, but they lack any objective standard for identifying the type of person who'd be likely to inspire trust. Similarly, they know they need candidates who are self-starters and highly motivated, but sales managers lack the skill to identify those characteristics during the interview process.

49

Sales managers are woefully aware of how bad they're failing when it comes to picking good candidates, according to Dr. Todd Harris, director of science at PI Worldwide. "Most sales managers estimate that only 40 percent to 60 percent of their current sales professionals are prepared to execute even the basic sales strategies," he says.

The situation is getting worse every year. For example, most sales managers are aware of the old 80/20 rule, which is that 80 percent of your revenue typically comes from 20 percent of the sales staff. However, research now shows that, on average, almost 87 percent of most companies' revenue comes from the top 13 percent of a company's sales performers, according to sales guru Mike Bosworth.

Sales managers can't pick top performers partly because they only have a vague notion why one sales professional sells five times as much as the person in the next office, using the same sales process and sales tools to sell the exact same product. The problem is so difficult that many sales managers seem to be in a state of helpless denial.

According to CSO Insights, a company that surveys and studies sales teams worldwide, only 4 in 10 firms systematically assess the basic competency of their sales candidates. Almost half of the firms surveyed felt their ability to "hire the right sales professionals" needed improvement, but only a measly 11 percent were planning to alter their hiring process.

Slapdash hiring creates unstable organizations that are constantly losing talent before their promise can be fulfilled. Astoundingly, annual sales representative turnover rates average approximately 30 percent, which means one out of three sales professionals is likely to leave the typical organization every year.

Now consider this: since the average turnover rate is 30 percent, that means many sales organizations suffer from attrition rates that are far higher. In fact, there are probably sales organizations out there that lose 9 out of 10 new hires within the first two years!

Needless to say, high turnover rates create a constant need for replacement personnel. And that's a big deal when it comes to making sales, because most companies report that it takes six months or longer to ramp up a new sales representative to full productivity.

And that figure is just for the average sales professional; fully replacing a top sales professional could easily take longer, if such replacement is even possible.

When it comes to hiring sales managers, the situation is even worse, if you can believe it. According to *SellingPower* magazine, the average tenure for a CSO or VP of Sales is now less than two years, barely long enough for the new executive to learn the ropes and begin to have an impact.

As you can well imagine, this constant churning of sales personnel costs money. A lot of money. General estimates vary but the rule of thumb is that turnover costs typically run anywhere between one and a half to two and a half times a person's base salary.

Part of that is direct costs (such as the cost of recruitment), but in the case of sales professionals can include additional costs, such as loss of customers, loss of contact information, and loss of credibility in customer accounts.

In short, lousy hiring results in lousy sales teams, which in turn means lower revenue. It's not too much to say that it's the root of most of the problems sales teams encounter when trying to sell in today's hypercompetitive environments.

How Most Companies Hire (and Why It Fails)

Let's look at how the typical company hires its sales team.

First, they send out a request for résumés, often with a newspaper ad or an Internet posting. The ad or post describes the position and a list of requirements, typically consisting of a number of years of experience in the same or a related field, a required level of education, and some desirable background traits. It might also include some vague (but essentially meaningless) requirements like "highly motivated."

Second, they have the HR group sort through the résumés to find the ones that match the requirements in the ad or post. This gets rid of the ones that are clearly inappropriate (e.g., written in crayon). The remainder are forwarded to the sales manager, who sticks them in a pile, then sorts them out using whatever criteria seems to make sense, or even one that doesn't (e.g., call the people who used colored paper last).

Third, the candidates are contacted for an initial interview where they'll be immediately judged based on what they're wearing and how they present themselves. Essentially, the interview is an audition for a sales call—even though the sales manager might be a very different sort of person from the typical customer to whom that candidate might eventually be selling.

To handle these interviews, sales managers typically develop what they believe to be an ideal profile that defines exactly what type of person is likely to succeed inside their organization. Then, they try to select candidates who match that profile. However, even an experienced sales manager can seize upon irrelevant details when trying to determine what creates sales success. For example, the coauthor of this book once worked with a sales manager who truly believed he could tell whether a candidate would be successful by the quality of the shine on his shoes.

During the interview, the sales manager asks a bunch of questions intended to elicit a better understanding of the candidate's personality. In most cases, the questions are predictable and trite, and have equally predictable and trite answers. The sales manager forms an opinion of the candidate based upon those answers, even though the candidate may have rehearsed them a dozen times and is delivering them like lines in a play.

Finally, the sales manager makes a best guess about who might work out, and then the fun begins. The scenario plays itself out in one of two ways:

Scenario 1: The firm trains the new hire in the firm's offerings, sales process and sales techniques, and sends the new hire out to sell. The new hire either makes his or her first numbers . . . or fails to do so. If the latter, the new hire is given further training and coaching until, finally, after about six months, it's pretty clear whether or not the new hire is going to work out.

Scenario 2: The firm throws the new hire into the job without any training, just to see whether he or she sinks or swims. In most cases, the new hire thrashes around and only manages to become productive by chance, even if he or she has the basic characteristics that, if properly developed, would make them successful in that selling environment.

Both scenarios result in one of three endgames:

Endgame 1: The new hire fails to thrive and thus is shown the door. The hiring firm loses the direct cost of training and orienting the new hire. The hiring firm also loses the revenue from sales that might have taken place had the right person been assigned to those accounts.

Endgame 2: The new hire fails to thrive but is allowed to remain. The hiring firm still loses everything in the previous endgame, but the pain continues on and on, for months, perhaps years. The dead weight of the nonperformer also becomes a drag on the rest of the organization.

Endgame 3: The new hire somehow manages to succeed but the sales manager has *absolutely no idea* why this particular candidate succeeded or how to replicate that success. Then the process starts all over again.

To make matters worse, there are many people, especially in sales, who are very talented at presenting themselves during job interviews as the ideal candidate, regardless of the job. The result can be a new hire that does not fit, which can cost many thousands of dollars in lost on-boarding costs, not to mention lost sales opportunities.

Given the circumstances, it's not surprising most companies keep hiring candidates who can't sell, or can't sell well. They're hiring candidates based entirely upon anecdotes and guess-work rather than science. Fortunately, there *is* a better way.

The Scientific Approach to Hiring

Traditional hiring approaches don't work because they're incredibly biased toward first impressions. In Malcolm Gladwell's book *What the Dog Saw and Other Adventures*,[1] he cites research showing that most hiring decisions are made actually within the first two or three seconds of meeting the person, and that such decisions are based, not upon a real understanding of whether the candidate will be effective at the job, but whether or not the candidate "feels right" for the job.

Unfortunately, the ability to create a quick bond with a hiring manager is not a particularly good indication of success at any particular job, even a sales job where first impressions are obviously important. The demands of today's sales positions are far too enormous to be satisfied by a nice smile and a firm handshake.

By contrast, with behavioral assessment, it's possible to build a statistical profile of the kind of person who is successful in your organization and then use a complimentary assessment to confirm whether a candidate is likely to thrive there. To do this, you first create a baseline of what works inside your organization, using a psychological testing tool that's been proven to be statistically valid by measuring key constructs

---

[1] (Little, Brown and Company, 2009).

such as the ability to self-start, the ability to take action in the face of adversity or obstacles, the ability to connect with and influence others, the ability to drive the right pace of activity, and so forth.

The most effective use of behavioral assessment in hiring takes place after candidates have made it past the first few gates of résumé check and a phone screen. The hiring manager asks the candidate to take a survey, and then combines the result of that candidate's survey with other data points (e.g., résumé, interview, references, experience level, etc.) to make a fully informed decision.

This allows a company to more accurately predict whether a candidate will prove effective at selling in that environment. In addition, psychological testing can and should be used post-hire as a component of sales management, coaching, and development efforts to motivate and maximize sales performance.

For example, PI Worldwide recently helped a company hire and assess a group of 32 outside sales representatives tasked with selling manufacturing equipment to medium-sized businesses. Psychological testing helped sales management cultivate sales professionals who were more independent, confident, assertive, and embracing of change. These individuals achieved over five times more sales volume during a 27-month period than those who did not have these characteristics.

Unlike job interviews and other recruiting methodologies, psychological testing is scientifically sound because it demonstrates both reliability and validity. It eliminates the guesswork and makes it easy to identify candidates who are likely to do well in any given selling environment. As a result, a much larger percentage of candidates become successful, and few, if any, sales professionals fail outright.

This also allows companies to hire right from the start. Behavioral assessment allows you to develop a process to consistently review what knowledge, skills, and abilities are needed for the role, while additionally ensuring that the candidate's personality is a fit for these requirements and with their potential teammates.

In other words, candidates who fall into the middle are offered a hope of improvement that's missing in the traditional hiring scenario. Since they are hired with a better knowledge of their basic psychological makeup, the sales manager can more easily customize training and coaching to match the way that candidate thinks and learns.

A major positive result of this is that candidates with great potential are far less likely to leave. For any sales organization, the departure of even a midperforming sales professional can have devastating economic consequences, such as the loss of customers who had close relationships with that individual.

How to Implement Scientific Hiring

There are seven steps to scientific hiring. Each step builds on the previous step in order to add a greater level of quantification into the hiring process, while removing much of the subjectivity that plagues most hiring efforts.

STEP 1: ANALYZE THE JOB

The key component to finding the best sales talent is to understand what you are looking for. Developing an accurate job description is mission one in effective hiring. Gaining input from several stakeholders can eliminate confusion and wasting time. A thorough job description should include the reporting structure, objectives of the role, the key performance indicators (KPIs), and experience and education requirements for the position.

In most cases, companies merely look at the educational or experiential requirements of a job in order to describe it. For example, a sales position in the semiconductor industry might require an electrical engineering degree and 10 years of experience. However, while those requirements are important, there are other elements that are just as important when it comes to determining whether a particular personality type is likely to be successful at any given job.

This analysis takes the form of statements such as: The job requires a lot of interaction with different types of customers. The job requires a lot of cold calling, either on the telephone or in person. The job requires the ability to connect quickly with new people. These elements then create a job profile or target to hire, which will naturally appeal to certain personality types who can be identified during the hiring process through the testing process.

In the PI system, this is accomplished using an instrument called Performance Requirement Options (PRO), which is used to define the requirements of a specific job and can be used to gain agreement by a group on the requirements of a job. In some cases, several PROs are completed by members of a team, managers, or board members and then discussed and compared to make a final PRO for a position. The PRO is expressed in a graphical format that allows for an easy comparison of the job profile to the characteristics of various job candidates.

For example, suppose you needed to hire somebody for an outside sales job with the following characteristics:

- The focus is on achieving results that are aligned with the larger picture of the organization and its strategic goals. This will require initiative, coupled with a sense of competitive drive, and the ability to stay focused on results despite changing conditions.
- Because environmental and organizational conditions change rapidly, the work involves innovation and creativity in generating ideas for quick response. Decision making will need to be focused on implementing practical, timely solutions. As a result, the job requires getting things done quickly and handling a variety of activities.

- The job requires self-assurance and the confidence to purposely drive toward results while constantly problem solving, and engaging the commitment of others is essential. The job will require a leadership style that is firm and goal oriented, and yet, most important, can also motivate, train, and engage others in an enthusiastic way. The emphasis on building rapport and relationships with individuals and groups requires an outgoing, poised, and persuasive communication style.

- Because the pace of the work is faster than average, the ability to learn quickly and thoroughly while continually recognizing and adapting to changing conditions is critical. The scope of the job requires effective delegation to proven people. Routine and repetitive details should be delegated, but with responsibility for follow-up and accountability for timely results.

- While the job requires the ability to act independently, a sense of urgency and the confidence to handle a variety of challenges, a full commitment to the success of the business and high standards of achievement are expected in this position.

- The emphasis is on results and effective systems that achieve results through and with people, rather than on the details of implementation. The job environment is flexible, constantly changing, and provides growth opportunity, recognition, and reward for the achievement of business results.

When translated into a PRO visual, this kind of job appears in Figure 4.1.

Please note that it's not necessary for you to understand why the PRO appears this way, because we're using it as an illustration of how scientific hiring works. (If you're interested in the specifics of the PRO and PI system, you should look into being certified on this system.) What's important here is

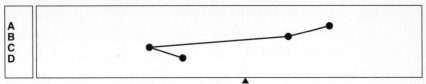

FIGURE **4.1**   Performance Requirement Options (PRO)

the general methodology for scientific hiring, not the specifics of the system that we're using for illustration purposes.

STEP 2: DESIGN AN APPROPRIATE RECRUITMENT AD

Once you've defined the environment in a way that can be matched to a personality profile, you write a recruitment ad that describes the environment—not the person. This is an important distinction because the purpose of the ad is to winnow out candidates from the very start who are unlikely to be successful in the position.

If you describe the characteristics of the person you'd like to hire, nearly everyone will think that they are appropriate for the job; just as everyone thinks they have a sense of humor, everyone thinks they are entrepreneurial or a self-starter or highly efficient. On the other hand, if you describe the environment, then the potential candidate will visualize working in the environment and find the notion of working there comfortable or uncomfortable based upon their reaction to the description.

For example, an ad that states a desire for a person who is "self-confident" will get far more inappropriate candidates than an ad that says "must remain eager to make sales, even after being rejected multiple times."

Here's an example:

- ◆ Before: "ABC Company would like to invite ambitious, hard-working individuals to apply for the position of full-time Outside Sales. Applicants should be able to bring new ideas and improvements to business practices, remain fair, respectful, and moral in all situations, and work well both independently and as part of a team. Contact us today for more information."

  ◆ After: "We are looking for a few strong individuals for full-time Outside Sales to join our fast-paced environment. This position gives you the ability to control your own destiny, have variety in your day, and be rewarded on your own results. Contact us today for more information."

Note that the major difference between the two ads is that the first describes the person, while the second describes the behavioral requirements of the job.

STEP 3: FILTER THE RÉSUMÉS

As you go through the résumés that respond to the tailored ad, you look for evidence (in each candidate's résumé) of the behaviors that will allow them to function effectively in the target environment. For example, if the environment requires a focus on process rather than goals, look for evidence in the résumé of patience, long-term thinking, and the ability to work through problems.

By contrast, if the environment requires extreme flexibility in terms of time management, look for evidence that the candidate has thrived in positions where there have been sudden changes. The result of this step will be a collection of résumés that already have a high likelihood of success.

For example, Figure 4.2 is a résumé that's been highlighted to identify elements that fit the PRO defined earlier. This résumé would clearly be a candidate to move to the next step.

In general, the top three or four items to scan on a résumé are:

  ◆ Years of experience in the role
  ◆ Number of jobs/length of time in each job
  ◆ Data that demonstrates success (e.g., grew sales 20 percent in the territory in the first year)

Mary J. Doe
50 Main Street, Anytown CT
MaryDoe@aol.com

OUTSIDE SALES EXECUTIVE / ACCOUNT MANAGER
Rapid Business Development • Market Opportunity Analysis

High-energy, customer-focused professional with stellar record of exceeding sales, profit, and market-share growth. Accomplished executive with exceptional record of motivating sales and operations teams through periods of rapid growth and change. Proven ability to quickly introduce new products and services to market, establishing strong market position.

CAREER HIGHLIGHTS

Business Development: Unparalleled record of boosting revenue and profit by identifying customer requirements and tailoring "best-in-class" solutions. Strong ability to recognize the most profitable way to position a product and identify the most lucrative markets and sectors.

Complex Sales Environments: Proven ability to uncover profitable opportunities, develop accurate forecasts, and help the buyer see the value in strong partnerships. Wide-ranging experience selling to the most reputable and revolutionary companies in the most competitive US and European markets.

Sales Awards: President's Club (Silver), 2003 • President's Club (Bronze), 2004. President's Club (Silver), 2005 & 2006 • "National Salesperson of the Year," 2008

PROFESSIONAL EXPERIENCE

ACME Worldwide Systems   2008–Present

Outside Sales Director
Generated record-breaking new business opportunities by employing cold-calling, referral, and other prospecting techniques to spark revenue growth. Provided hands-on leadership and ongoing management for high-profile campaigns that built visibility and quickly increased revenue.

(continued)

FIGURE 4.2   Résumé Under Review

- *Tripled revenue in 9 months by acquiring 22 new accounts, exceeding sales goals by 73 percent.*
- *Grew account base 31 percent and successfully launched 12 new product lines across multiple distribution channels.*
- *Expanded account base 40 percent over 2 years by developing focused business plan for territory and aggressively following all leads.*
- *Grew revenue in the Northeast region by 80 percent from previous year and landed more than 25 new Fortune 1000 accounts in 2008.*
- *Consistently ranked number one in monthly sales, maintaining a national rank in the top 10 for 8 years running.*

FIGURE 4.2 Résumé Under Review (*continued*)

It's from résumés like this that you build your list of candidates.

STEP 4: CONDUCT TELEPHONE INTERVIEWS

This step is important because interviewing by telephone removes some of the first impression bias that so frequently ends up with inappropriate hiring. During the telephone interview, look for further evidence of the behaviors that will work in the target environment. At the same time, probe deeply into one or two areas to make certain that the candidate has been genuine on his or her résumé.

An early interview typically includes a short telephone call to screen candidates and determine if they are viable for the next step. A first call typically includes questions like:

- Tell me a little about your job search?
- Help me understand what you are looking for?
- Describe what caught your eye about our opportunity?
- Describe the ideal sales job from your perspective?
- How would your prior sales managers describe your sales capabilities? For business development? For enhancing existing customer business?
- Describe the ideal sales support you would need to be most effective? What was the worst sales role you have been engaged in?

- ◆ What does the customer mean to you?
- ◆ What does servicing the sale mean to you?
- ◆ Why do you want to work for this company?

During this step, you're looking for signs that the candidate possesses the abilities and temperament to fulfill the requirements defined in the PRO. The result of this brief screening is a short list of candidates to be seriously considered.

STEP 5: GIVE THE CANDIDATES A BEHAVIOR ASSESSMENT

In this step, you use a scientifically valid instrument as a measurement tool to determine, without bias, how well the candidate's core personality matches the job requirements for that position and environment.

During this process, you consider all the key elements of data including résumé, references, expertise, and behavioral assessment. This allows you to eliminate candidates who are clearly wrong for the position, and prioritize forward the candidates who most closely match the desired personality types fit for the job.

As an example, we'll turn once again to the outside sales job described in Step 1. In the PI system, candidates for the position are given a behavioral assessment that measures the drives and motivations of each individual. In the PI system, the scoring produces a graphic behavioral pattern that allows the company to easily compare the PRO (Figure 4.3) of the position with the PI of the candidate.

FIGURE **4.3** The PRO

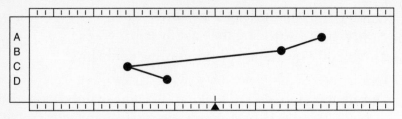

FIGURE **4.4**   Candidate A

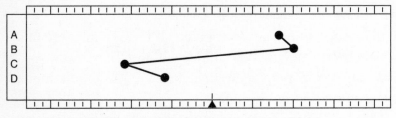

FIGURE **4.5**   Candidate B

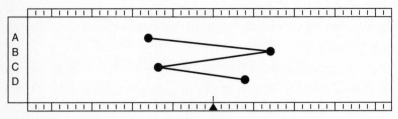

FIGURE **4.6**   Candidate C

Candidate A shows what, in the PI system, is called an "Authoritative Management Pattern." As you can see visually, this is a very strong behavioral fit between the position and the person.

Candidate B shows what's known as a "Persuasive Sales Pattern." This graphic shows that there is a strong fit with a few distinctions worth investigating during the interview process to make sure this is a long-term fit.

Candidate C shows what's known as an "Altruistic Pattern." The differences in the needs of the job from the needs of the person are probably too large for this to be a fit.

Candidates A and B continue onto the next step, while Candidate C—despite having a strong résumé and having passed the telephone screen—is dropped from the process.

STEP 6: CONDUCT STRATEGIC INTERVIEWS

To select the best candidates from among those who match well or are within an exceptable range, you personally interview and ask questions to confirm the viability of the candidate and to explore any fits or gaps. For example, the person may be self-motivated, connects quickly with others, and follows rules and process well; however, the job requires them to possess patience and they have a very high sense of urgency.

By probing into the gap, you know in advance how to manage the rep rather than having them leave because the demands of the job are too slow paced in their opinion. Having the candidate elaborate on their past work experiences gives you insight into how easy or hard any gaps are to bridge.

In practice, based on the three situations posed in Step 5, you would approach the interview process differently.

For example, Candidate A is behaviorally a very strong fit, so the majority of the questions you would ask would be around other criteria such as what is motivating their job change. You ask questions like:

- Tell me what prompted your job search?
- Describe the kind of environment you are looking for?
- What is most important to you as you evaluate this position?

Candidate B is within the range of viable candidates but you would leverage the interview process to tease out the fits and gaps. This person connects quickly with others, is motivated by social interaction, and is flexible in the approach to process; however, the job requires a bit more independence and focused on tasks. Your questions need to see how the person would flourish in your company, like so:

- ◆ You work well with others and connect quickly, tell me how you approach the sales role where you are working independently?
- ◆ Describe the sales process that you used in your previous role?
- ◆ Give me an example of a situation where you took the initiative and started something new?

After a series of these interviews, you will likely find several (or at least one) candidate who is highly likely to be successful at the job. The likelihood that the person you hire will not thrive is far lower than would be the case using traditional hiring methods.

STEP 7: REFINE THE MODEL

Since jobs tend to evolve over time, a PRO may need to be changed periodically as well. Over time, these measurements form an increasingly predictable picture of how an individual will behave in specific situations. When reviewed by a trained PI analyst, these measurements can be used to assess and predict how an individual will fit the behavioral requirements of a job.

Case Study

RAINSOFT

Rainsoft is an Illinois-based company that previously sold and installed water treatment systems through a network of approximately 200 independent dealerships around the world. In 2005, the company needed to make a major change in its sales model, a change that would require the cultivation of different skill sets throughout the sales team.

In order to grow its business, Rainsoft agreed to be acquired by the private equity firm Waud Capital Partners. One of the first initiatives of the newly formed company was to expand their existing dealership franchise model to include company stores that would be owned and managed by Rainsoft corporate.

This change in strategy would theoretically allow Rainsoft to penetrate high potential markets where they had previously been unable to find an independent distributor. In embarking on this new business model, Rainsoft realized that employee turnover would be a challenge, since turnover had continued to plague their independent dealers.

This was a significant issue for the firm because the process of on-boarding new employees involved considerable expense. Prior to starting at a dealership, all new employees were required to attend a 7-day product training course led by the general managers and the corporate training staff. Unfortunately, the newly trained hires would often leave within 30 to 60 days resulting in a loss of productivity, profitability, and morale for both the dealership and the corporate training team.

When Andrea Herran, the new director of HR at Rainsoft, learned of the retention issue in the stores, she knew there had to be a better way to find the right people for the key positions in the corporately owned stores. Andrea became aware of behavioral assessment and investigated its use to help with the challenges of hiring and retention.

To launch its use in Rainsoft, she and key members of her staff and the field team (recruiters and trainers) were trained to administer and interpret the PI survey.

(continued)

(*continued*)

Together with a PI consultant, they developed profiles of the behavioral requirements for each of the dealership positions.

The concept of using behavioral assessment in hiring was not well received at first. Many of the hiring managers had been with the company for over 10 years and had been challenged by consistent turnovers, but were nevertheless skeptical about the ability of behavioral assessment to address the issue.

Rather than push the issue, Rainsoft's top management decided to let the tool speak for itself. For the next six months, all potential new hires took a behavioral assessment prior to the interview. The results would be discussed with the hiring managers along with recommendations, but ultimately the managers would make the final hiring decision.

It soon became clear that behavioral assessment was a better predictor of sales success (and a consequently low turnover) than the gut feeling of the hiring managers. For example, one Rainsoft recruiter wanted to hire a salesperson based on their professional experience and strong interview, even though the candidate's results on the behavioral assessment were not a strong fit for the sales position.

The recruiter felt strongly that the candidate was the right person for the job and hired him. However, within a short period of time it was apparent that the employee was struggling and ultimately left the company. "In this situation the results of the Predictive Index revealed this individual focused on a high level of detail which, in this type of business, translates into difficulty closing the sale," explains Herran.

The company subsequently changed its hiring policy so that the hiring team will not move forward with a candidate without the insight from the behavioral assessment. "If the candidate is not a strong fit for the job, we do not hire them [because] it's not worth it," says Herran. "The people we hired in support of their PI results are still with us today [while] the other people left shortly after they were hired, many within 30 days."

Case Study

CENTIER BANK

Since 1895, Centier Bank has been a family-owned and managed financial service provider. The current president, Michael E. Schrage, is the fourth generation to oversee the daily operations of the bank. With 44 branch locations, Centier is currently serving in more than 22 communities with about 700 associates and more than $1.9 billion in assets.

Schrage wanted to develop a strategic process to attract the best talent and build a culture founded on the values of integrity, respect, friendship, caring, and loyalty. During a conversation with a colleague discussing the direct impact talented employees had on customer relationships and company performance, he learned of the PI behavioral assessment tool.

After experiencing the PI firsthand, Schrage made the commitment to use the PI for all hiring, including the use of the PRO to define the requirements of the job in behavioral

(continued)

(*continued*)

terms. The bank's HR department created a PRO job profile for each position at the bank, and compared the PIs for each person with the PRO. At the same time, anyone who managed people (the executive team, branch managers, and department managers) attended the PI Management Workshop where they were trained in analyzing the PI information.

Taking a scientific approach to hiring was particularly important for Centier because being so close to major cities such as Indianapolis and Chicago tends to make hiring quality people difficult, according to Schrage. This makes it even more important to focus on making a strong hire right from the start and developing these employees for peak retention.

By using the insight from the PI to tailor their interview questions, the bank's hiring manager and HR group were able to determine the best fit for the job and for the culture of the bank. In 1992, turnover at the bank was at 17 percent to 20 percent. Today, Centier Bank boasts a rate of 10 percent, which is significantly lower than the regional and state averages.

In fact, Centier Bank also has more people today with 10-plus years with the bank than at any time in its history. Not coincidently, Centier Bank has been named Best Place to Work by the Indiana Chamber of Commerce for three consecutive years, moving up in the ratings every year: the first year ranking number 10, the year after that number 5, and for 2009, they achieved the number 4 spot for large companies in Indiana.

5

The Science of Sales Training

I have been in the training business for the past 22 years. In 2006, I took the SSAT and scored a 62 percent. I concluded that the test was really dumb because I thought I knew the right answers and the questions weren't good questions. I picked up the phone and called Nancy to complain. She chuckled and then explained, based on my skill profile, exactly how I sell things. I was amazed. It was like she'd been on sales calls with me. I went through CFS training with Nancy, and the first year my gross revenue went up 20 percent and I broke into the top five sales reps for my firm for the first time.

—Dave O'Brien, Associate, The Predictive Group

Sales training is a huge business. In the United States alone, companies that sell business-to-business spend between $4 and $7 billion on sales training, according to Dave Stein, CEO of ES Research, a company that studies the sales training market. About 60 percent of that amount is spent on in-house training (product updates, marketing training, etc.) while the rest is spent hiring outside trainers to help sales teams become more effective.

Given that level of yearly expenditure, that sales training would be massively increasing the ability of sales teams to sell. Unfortunately, that's usually not the case. "Nine out of ten companies say that the sales team, after training, doesn't end up with any lasting value," says Stein. The problem lies, not in the training itself, but rather in the traditional methods that sales managers use to buy sales training. As with hiring sales talent, a scientific approach yields much better results.

Why Sales Training Fails

Sales training has a long and checkered history, with problems that have continued to ripple through today's sales organizations. Until the advent of the solution selling model in the 1970s (and even afterward), sales managers widely assumed that successful selling behavior could be reproduced through the use of ritual behaviors.

The goal for many tactical sales training programs was to make selling as predictable as possible. The training was designed to ensure that everyone on the sales team spoke, acted, looked, and even moved in the exact same manner, in the mistaken belief that customers would react identically to the same stimuli.

As we learned in the chapter on skill assessment, the concept of ritualized sales behavior was generally ineffective. The problem was twofold.

First, the sales rituals themselves were not based upon research but largely upon speculation about what ought to work based upon an individual salesperson's behavior. However, as we saw in the previous chapter, different types of personalities and temperaments are suited to different types of sales jobs, making the concept of a "one-size-fits-all" an impossibility.

Second, the sales rituals that actually worked under certain, limited circumstances (e.g., "but wait, there's more!") quickly slipped into the lexicon of popular culture. As a result, an increasing number of potential customers became able to identify the standard sales techniques and, more importantly, view them as being sleazy and unethical.

For example, the actor W.C. Fields, in movies like *You Can't Cheat an Honest Man* (1939) and *Never Give a Sucker an Even Break* (1941) lampooned the stock character of the carnival pitchman. While Field's sales pitches in those films seem, to a modern viewer, to be ridiculously over the top, they are in fact nearly identical to ritualized sales pitches given as examples in serious sales training films, such as those by early sales trainer Elmer Wheeler ("Don't sell the steak, sell the sizzle!") and dozens of "how to sell a car" shorts by industrial filmmaker Jam Handy.

The continued failure of these sales rituals to produce sales results (in anything more than a haphazard fashion) had an interesting impact on sales culture. To the public at large (and even to the sales community, to a lesser degree) a career in sales became increasingly viewed as both futile and depressing. The apotheosis of this viewpoint was Arthur Miller's Pulitzer Prize-winning 1949 play *Death of a Salesman*, which essentially documents an entire family's attempt to avoid a sales career, even to the point of committing suicide.

The pop culture view of sales, though exaggerated, wasn't entirely off base. Sales in these traditional environments was grueling, and inevitably involved massive amounts of rejection. However, even though sales professionals in general, and sales managers in particular, were well aware that sales rituals didn't often work, there was no obvious alternative. As a result, sales training remained focused on ritual one-size-fits-all behaviors.

Rather than changing the content of sales training so that it would be more effective, sales organizations focused on helping individuals cope with the constant rejection by adding motivational training to the mix. The idea behind motivation training was, of course, to keep spirits up, even when (and especially when) the sales numbers went down.

Since sales professionals were being asked, from the start, to take a leap of faith that ritual behaviors would result in success, it's not surprising that much of the early forms of sales training had a distinctly religious flavor. Dale Carnegie, Napoleon Hill, and Norman Vincent Peale all promoted, if not a specific religion, at least a certain level of religiosity as being crucial to sales success.

The combination of sales ritual with motivational training was not always enlightened or positive in nature, though. In the 1992 movie *Glengarry Glen Ross* (based on the play by David Mamet that won a 1984 Tony and Pulitzer Prize), a hot-shot sales trainer, memorably played by Alec Baldwin, is brought in by top management to motivate the discouraged troops. In a much-quoted speech, the trainer provides both the ritualized bromides (e.g., "A.B.C.—Always Be Closing") and also crude motivation (e.g., "Coffee is for closers!").

While the movie is fictional, it remains popular among sales professionals because many, if not most, have been exposed to similarly inept sales training in real life. Indeed, ritualized sales training, combined with rah-rah motivation is far from extinct.

Quite the contrary. It is still, for instance, possible to purchase seminars based upon Elmer Wheeler's cartoonish sales techniques as well as a version of every sales training fad that's entered the business world over the past 70 years. Motivational training is a huge segment of the overall sales training industry, with top speakers commanding five- and six-figure speaking fees.

While many sales gurus are simply repackaging or refurbishing the same tired material, others are adding their own wrinkles. The result is a sales training industry that's largely been dominated by a series of fads rather than measurable improvement. "What happens a lot is that a CSO in an airport picks up the latest and greatest business book and reads it on the flight, and decides, then and there, that this is exactly what the sales team needs to be successful," Stein explains. "He calls the author, they hit it off, and he hires the author to train the sales staff."

What happens then is entirely predictable. The author comes, gives a seminar, and gets everyone pumped up. Then the sales team goes off and tries to use whatever techniques were taught and finds out that they don't work in real life. Salespeople get a signed copy of a book and a few ideas that didn't prove useful. "Then the CSO does the same thing again, with a different author," says Stein. "It's 'flavor of the month' and the poor sales guys end up feeling like their time is constantly being wasted by training that doesn't make any sense."

Why Sales Training Doesn't Get Measured

This is not to say that all sales training is useless. Far from it. Many sales training courses contain content that, under the right circumstances, might prove useful, according to Stein. However, such training rarely proves effective because it does not match the needs of the individual or the needs of the sales team in general. So, while a particular sales training program might generate a minor improvement in one area of the sales process, that improvement is often insignificant compared to the time and expense of the training.

For example, suppose a sales team is deployed in an industry, like retail, where most of the purchasing is done by professional buyers. In this environment, a sales training seminar designed for selling solutions to software companies would probably be confusing rather than useful. Similarly, a company where the bulk of the lead generation comes from a website is likely to find a seminar on cold calling to simply be wasted effort.

Such mismatches are surprisingly common, according to Stein, because companies are often clueless about how their customers prefer to buy. "Most vice presidents of sales think they know what works, but when customers are interviewed, there are often huge disconnects between what the executives think should work and how customers actually buy," he explains.

Even when companies know how their customers buy, they may end up investing in training that simply enhances a strength, while leaving revenue-killing weaknesses in place. For example, suppose a company is generating all sorts of hot leads with a winning telesales program, but is having trouble closing those leads after they've been generated. In this case, spending training dollars to make the telesales group more effective will simply result in a larger number of hot leads that never get closed.

In many cases, these mismatches are never surfaced due to a lack of scientific measurement. As a result, it's often impossible to tell whether or not a particular sales training effort has been successful or not.

This is not to say that sales trainers don't encourage the use of metrics. However, in many cases, they promote the use of metrics that guarantee that the sales training will get the credit if sales go up, and something (or someone) else will get the blame should sales go down.

For example, many sales training programs tout high customer satisfaction as measured by course evaluations. Such evaluations, however, often measure whether the instructor was entertaining, rather than the actual impact of the sales training, in terms making the team more effective at selling.

Another common way of measuring sales training is to look at whether sales revenue increased for the group after the sales training has taken place. This type of measurement isn't irrelevant, but unless other factors are removed from the mix, such as general economic conditions, changes in product mix, and so forth, the actual impact of the sales training will simply be obscured by the impact of these other factors.

It's theoretically possible, of course, to build measurement models comparing the performance of similar groups (or individuals) selling into similar markets, one group trained and the other not. In practice, however, this is seldom done, either because it's difficult to find groups that are easily comparable or because there is pressure (from the sales trainers and often from sales management) to train everybody.

Some sales training organizations measure compliance— checking to see whether or not sales employees are actually executing the behaviors that they've been trained to execute. This is not necessarily a bad idea, if done honestly, and if there's reason to believe that executing those behaviors will actually increase sales productivity.

However, measuring compliance can also provide a convenient scapegoat for the failure of the sales training. Mike Bosworth admitted to the coauthor of this book that he was accustomed to blaming the pigheadedness of sales personnel when they failed to embrace solution selling after they'd been trained, rather than attributing noncompliance to the sensible abandonment of sales techniques that were proving ineffective when implemented in actual sales situations.

The simple truth is that many sales training executives shy away from scientifically valid measurement because they realize, at some level, that their sales training methods won't survive close scrutiny. It makes more financial sense (from the perspective of sales trainers who want to sell more seminars and programs) to keep measurement ambiguous.

Similarly, it's often in the interests of the sales managers who hired the trainers to espouse a measurement system that virtually guarantees that the decision to hire that firm will appear, to top management, to have been a sound investment. The situation is similar to what occurs with large Information Technology (IT) projects, where the IT vendor and their customer IT management collude to hide project failures in order to provide mutual protection, respectively, against loss of revenue and loss of employment!

The irony of the situation is that, if valid, scientific measurement were the rule rather than the exception, it would very quickly become clear (both to sales management and top management) that training that combines ritualized tactics and motivation is ineffective and outmoded. Scientific measurement would also quickly uncover situations where sales training (under other circumstances) might be useful, but (under current circumstances) is ineffective.

Scientific Measurement versus Conventional Wisdom

Surprising perspectives frequently emerge when sales training is actually measured scientifically. For example, a major trend in sales training is the presentation of materials in an online environment. The assumption behind this trend is that busy sales professionals are more likely to absorb and incorporate sales training if they can do so at their own pace and when it's convenient for them.

In addition, the theory says that online sales training is more likely to be accessed because it is presented in the same convenient environment (like an iPad) that sales reps use for consuming entertainment content. Unfortunately, while that theory seems to make sense, based upon the popular conception of how today's professionals work and learn, it also happens to be utter nonsense.

The Aberdeen Group, one of the country's most respected high-tech research organizations, recently published research from surveys conducted at over 500 companies. That study laid out the following reasons why sales organizations pursue sales training:

1. Increase revenue (70 percent)
2. Align sales activity with business objectives (40 percent)

3. Create more meaningful sales conversations (53 percent)
4. Enhance skills in prospecting, nurturing, and closing (49 percent)

No surprises there. However, the survey also revealed that the kind of training that companies want (as shown in items 3 and 4) are most effective when taught in a classroom environment rather than online. According to the study, among all companies that deploy external training solutions, those favoring instructor-led methodologies show an average 14 percent increase in the percentage of sales reps achieving their annual quota, compared to those that do not utilize this delivery modality.

According to Aberdeen, there are two primary reasons that instructor-led sales training is more effective. (See Figure 5.1.) First, despite the fact that a great deal of sales communication takes place through online media, like e-mail, sales-oriented learning remains a highly personal and interactive process. Second, it turns out that an expert-level professional communicator/coach is more likely to provide insight, instruction, and

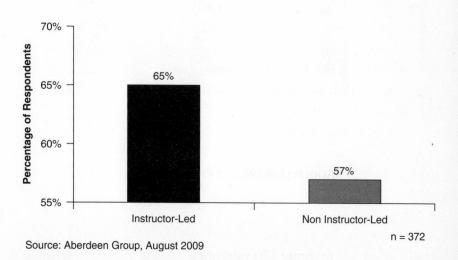

Source: Aberdeen Group, August 2009

n = 372

Figure 5.1 Percentage of Sales Reps Achieving Quota

reinforcement of best practices for sales representatives and their leaders.

In other words, much of the sales training investment that companies have made in online methodologies has probably been either wasted entirely, or spent ineffectively. This is not to say that all online sales training is entirely useless, of course. However, when measured scientifically, it becomes clear that for the people-oriented sales skills, classroom training is statistically more useful.

The Aberdeen study revealed another interesting fact: that companies that utilize instructor-led sales training are twice as likely (as those that do not) to have a process in place to reinforce the methodology in the field, as shown in the graph in Figure 5.2.

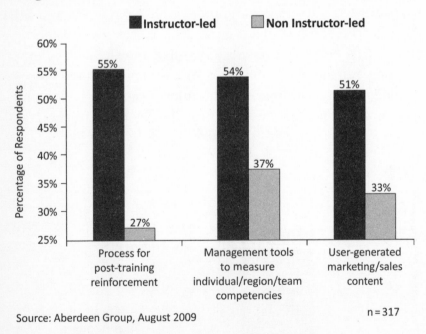

FIGURE 5.2 Capabilities that Support and Reinforce Sales Training

These results are counterintuitive because presenting the training online offers opportunities to check, for example, whether individual sales reps have accessed a given training program. However, such mechanistic measurements only reflect whether an individual has viewed a program, not whether or not the contents of that program are being used effectively.

As we can see from the Aberdeen study, the scientific measurement of sales training can produce results that run contrary to conventional wisdom and can effectively debunk sales training fads. Unfortunately, studies like the Aberdeen survey achieve scientific validity by studying multiple companies, a methodology that's not practical for measuring sales training internal to a single company. For that, you need a somewhat more subtle instrument.

Applying Science to Sales Training

Ideally, a sales training program should be implemented only after you've researched how your customers want to buy, and assessed the ability of the current sales team to address that group of customers, according to Stein. "Only then can you know what needs to change in order to sell more effectively," he explains.

Customized training is important because it's challenging to implement real behavioral change in an organization. "It requires not just research and customization to ensure relevance, but also a program of monitoring, measuring, and reinforcement, which is why the 'flavor of the month' sales training programs usually prove useless," he explains. While some basic sales skills (like establishing a relationship, assessing needs, providing a solution, etc.) are valuable in nearly every sales environment, increasing sales in a specific environment generally involves precisely targeting the training to the unique situation.

A critical missing element in sales training is a deep understanding of what skills each rep is entering the training with. Often the only measurement watched by sales managers is actual sales results. Those numbers, while obviously important, unfortunately provide very little insight into what training is or isn't needed. The scientific approach adds measurement to the process and looks at the correlation between sales skills and actual sales results.

Ideally, sales training should be measured on a variety of different levels, each approaching the impact of the training from a different aspect, as shown in Figure 5.3.[1]

LEVEL of OBJECTIVES	FOCUS of OBJECTIVES
Level 1 Reaction/Satisfaction	Defines a specific level of satisfaction and reaction to the training/coaching as it is delivered to the participants.
Level 2 Learning	Defines specific knowledge and skill(s) to be developed/acquired by training/coaching participants.
Level 3 Application/Implementation	Defines behavior that must change as the knowledge and skills are applied in the work setting following the delivery of the training/coaching.
Level 4 Business Impact	Defines the specific business measures that will change or improve as a result of the application of the training/coaching.
Level 5 Return on Investment (ROI)	Defines the specific return on investment from the implementation of the training/coaching, comparing costs with benefits.

FIGURE 5.3   Levels of Objectives for Measuring Training

Most sales training measurement schemes remain incomplete because they fail to test levels 2 and 3, thereby making it more difficult to correctly interpret levels 4 and 5.

The scientific approach therefore starts by benchmarking each rep's current skills, prior to training. For example, at PI Worldwide, we use the SSAT web-based assessment to provide benchmark data that allows sales management to

---

[1]Jack Phillips and Ron Stone. *How to Measure Training Results* (New York: McGraw-Hill, 2002), p 39.

better strategize, plan, and execute their sales interventions. The SSAT provides data on three levels—the sales force, the group (defined by the client; i.e., geography, title, etc.), and the individual. This concrete data gives the sales management a clear statistical picture of the sales skills of their organization, teams, and people.

The net effect of this kind of assessment is to demystify sales results and turn it from a "black box" into something that can be changed, adjusted, and improved. This is important, because sales managers who lack these metrics often make wildly incorrect guesses about what is working, or will work, within their sales organizations.

Measurement and evaluation are a sales manager's best ammunition to guarantee value from their sales training investments. Ideally, this process should be rolled out as an eight-step process:

Step 1: Administer a skills benchmark. Prior to training, examine current skills, identify group-wide weaknesses and strengths, and compare to the requirements of the sales jobs in the organization.

Step 2: Customize the training. Based upon the *group* results of STEP 1, build a customized sales training program (or programs) that leverages strengths and shores up weaknesses.

Step 3: Customize the coaching. Based upon the *individual* results of STEP 1, build a customized sales coaching plan for each individual in the group, assuming attendance of the sales training. (We'll discuss coaching in the next chapter.)

Step 4: Train the team. Execute the customized sales training for the entire team or teams.

Step 5: Execute the coaching. Based on the results of STEP 3, reinforce that training for each individual. (We'll discuss coaching in the next chapter.)

Step 6: Remeasure skills. Six to twelve months after the customized training, retest sales skills to determine what's sticking and where additional training or coaching might be needed.

Step 7: Provide additional training and/or coaching.

Step 8: Remeasure skills against benchmark. Twelve to twenty-four months after initial benchmark, retest skills and compare them to the benchmark to track progress.

Needless to say, all measurement should be in conjunction with actual sales results, paying close attention to the relationship between the cognitive (skills knowledge) and results (execution of that knowledge).

As you can see, possessing scientific data about the performance of the sales team is crucial to planning effective (and cost-effective) sales training interventions. When sales managers can see statistics across all reps, they have a better and more solid view of the strengths and areas of growth.

This process often involves a certain amount of surprise. For example, the Chief Learning Officer (CLO) for a global PR agency in New York City, once called PI Worldwide looking for a one-day sales program on presentation skills for their top 100 account managers around the world.

He expressed that their industry was hard hit by the economy, that buyers were tougher, ROI demonstration requests constant, and the ability to gain new clients had become extremely competitive. The author asked one simple question: "How do you know they need training on presentation skills?" His response: "Well, that's what they asked for."

In other words, the chief learning officer was assuming that the account manager staff was self-aware enough (both as a group and as individuals) to understand their own strengths and weaknesses. However, as we'll discover in the next chapter, individuals are often no more able to diagnose sales problems than sick people are able to diagnose diseases.

In this case, after further discussion, the chief learning officer agreed to verify the reasonability of the request by administering the SSAT to this core group of 100. The results came out differently than expected (Figure 5.4).

	Open	Investigate	Present	Confirm	Position
All Company	3.0	1.0	4.0	2.0	2.0

FIGURE 5.4   SSAT Results

The results showed the highest score of 4.0 to be in the Present area of the SSAT—the exact area where the account team had requested training. By contrast, the two related skills: investigate (asking questions) at 1.0 and confirm (getting a yes) at 2.0 were quite low. This was the real reason that the group was having trouble increasing sales.

These weaknesses were even negatively impacting their strength! Although this group was quite savvy at presenting, their presentations were not targeted enough because they had limited information about the customer, due to their lack of questioning skills. In addition, without that key information around decision making, buying criteria, and how they were being evaluated—their presentations, while quite polished, tended to fall flat.

More importantly, even when the presentation went well, the typical account manager in this group lacked the skills to ask for the business and get a yes.

As the result of scientific testing, the CLO requested an entirely different kind of training. Rather than a one-day sales program on presentation skills, they rolled out a two-day program that leveraged their strong presentation skills by building up the surround skills. The increase in these surround skills was, of course, measurable, allowing management to clearly see where the training had been effective and allowing them to do follow-on coaching more effectively.

Not surprisingly, the overall results from that group of 100 account managers around the world was an increase in business of 18 percent that year for the firm, in a very tough economy. In other words, the scientific data gave them the statistics to leverage the strengths of the organization and provide the missing ingredients for sales growth.

Customizing Sales Training

A key concept in the eight-step process described earlier is the customization of the sales training.

Some sales training companies provide only an off-the-shelf option for their training, especially when the training is done in a public setting or with a variety of attending companies. Other sales training companies promise customization, but actually provide an off-the-shelf program, perhaps with sample customers taken from the audience's customer base.

The problem with off-the-shelf sales training is such programs, even when the skills taught are appropriate, put the burden on the audience to translate the teaching into something that's really useful.

The real goal of customization is to make sure that every minute of a sales rep's time in sales training is relevant. Any sales training you bring to your team should ideally deliver value and content that can be applied immediately to their day-to-day behavior, by adapting it to their world in advance. This is a five-step process:

STEP 1: SKILLS ASSESSMENT

Prior to the training, administer a skills assessment (e.g., an SSAT) to all reps to examine the current skill profile at three levels: (1) the overall sales force, (2) the specific sales group, and (3) each individual sales rep. The CSO or sales VP uses the sales force-level data to select and delimit general sales skills that will be taught companywide. The sales manager uses the group-level data to understand the strengths and weaknesses of the group, and thus prepares for helping the group to improve performance. Each participant then uses his or her individual-level data to understand their specific skills and to help them focus on what will be most valuable for them to learn.

STEP 2: RESEARCH INTERVIEWS

Interview about four or five reps for about 20 minutes each to hear in their own words about the state of affairs. Ideally, you should select a mix of top producers, middle of the road, and strugglers, because the cross section helps identify what's going on at each level of performance. During the interview, ask the reps a series of questions about their current situation, the marketplace, the barriers they perceive, and what they hope to get out of a sales training program. Such conversations tend to be packed with insightful and powerful information to help the customization program.

STEP 3: RESEARCH SURVEY

In addition to the one-on-one conversations, it's useful to ask the same questions of every participant in the program via an e-mail survey. Ideally, this should be done in such a way that it encourages confidentiality. The survey data is helpful in confirming the assumptions made by management, verifying trends, and identifying new information. The group data is then combined with the individual interviews and skills assessment data to provide a complete picture of the current situation.

STEP 4: REVIEW FINDINGS

When the previous three steps are complete, review the data with the management team, and adjust the training program to reflect that data. Armed with the data, the sales training provider is now prepared to make all skill areas relevant and useful to the participants of the sales training program. *Note*: In some cases, that data may contain some surprises for management, or surface issues that aren't amenable to sales training. For example, the interview calls may reveal a big issue with morale or around compensation. However, identifying the challenge gives management a chance to address the issues rather than detract from the training.

STEP 5: CREATE A CASE SCENARIO

Have an instructional designer interview Subject Matter Experts (SMEs) who have an in-depth knowledge of the industry that the audience sells to. When those interviews are complete, the instructional designer writes an industry-specific and client-specific scenario that is relevant to the skills that are to be taught. Each area of the scenario provides an opportunity for participants to learn skills, practice the skills, and apply them to a realistic situation. While this step is optional, experience says that this deeper level and degree of customization enhances the learner's experience and increases overall skills retention.

Case Study

THE CLARK-MORTENSON AGENCY

The Clark-Mortenson Agency (CMA) is one of the largest independently owned insurance and financial services agencies in northern New England offering a range of specialties including employee benefits, commercial property, general liability, worker's compensation, worksite market programs, and bonds.

Since its inception in 1877, the company has worked to develop its strong reputation and brand recognition to grow its sales. However, with increasing economic pressures, it realized that it needed to maximize the effectiveness of the sales teams.

At CMA, the sales team includes 10 outside producers and four inside salespeople who approach each sale as a collaborative effort within the agency. The company takes a holistic approach to solving clients' needs and goals, rather than focusing on just one aspect of the client's insurance or benefits needs.

To create a successful long-term strategy, the company has been creating a more self-aware sales team using data-driven assessment tools and customer-focused sales training to successfully shift the sales focus away from the products Clark-Mortenson had to offer to identifying and meeting the needs of the client.

The agency now incorporates Customer-Focused Selling into its sales training in multiple locations across the company and discovered an effective way to improve individual performance, increase sales team productivity, create predictable, sustainable sales results, and help its people grow professionally within the company.

(*continued*)

(*continued*)

The agency is well-known and has a strong reputation; however, it was not realizing the level of new business sales needed to continue to grow in the marketplace. It had established a number of new services, including compliance and HR assistance, online resources for top clients, and a seminar series, just to name a few. Even with those new client-focused services, it needed a better way to get in front of prospects and elevate its closing ratio.

The company turned to scientifically proven data-based assessment tools paired with individualized sales training. Every salesperson completed a web-based assessment, which provided each producer with a very specific overview to determine his or her current strengths and areas of growth, which were then addressed with a training course.

Assessment tools like these can help a sales team to look in the mirror and challenge traditional thinking. The company found that it improved its approach to prospective clients, how producers interact with them, and how to gain consensus to finalize the sale.

Case Study

YANKEE CANDLE

The Yankee Candle Company is the largest premium candle manufacturer in the United States. According to Dorrin Exford, the company's director of learning and development, in 2000, Yankee Candle had no formal training department for its then 1,500-employee staff.

More recently, when Michael Thorne joined in 2006 as SVP Wholesale, Yankee Candle had just embarked on a significant market-facing change: "With a shift in our business model from gift-oriented to selling through national retail accounts," Thorne says, "we had to move from reactive to solution-providing support for our customers."

Exford had deployed the Predictive Index assessment tools since early 2002, to help Yankee Candle identify the optimal individuals within the hiring process, as well as to create more effective teams, but now the company is engaged in B2B Customer-Focused Selling for the first time.

As a result, the 80-person wholesale division—not just sales, but merchandising, finance, and planning staffers—were formally trained in Customer-Focused Selling methodologies. The PI and SSAT tools provided useful insight to understand the salesperson's natural behavior style and to be aware of the need to adjust it according to the style and needs of internal and external customers.

Exford explains, "We started by using these tools to identify our star players, those who had the natural skill to sell, align behavior to build relationships easily, to analyze and ask investigative questions. We benchmarked the starting place of each participant and will reevaluate in a year. Our star players identified will become our standard future performers."

(*continued*)

(*continued*)

According to Thorne, "We used actual customer case studies for our customer-focused training program, and through role-playing in class, we worked to find solutions to meet the customer's needs. It made it real, and we solved problems while learning."

The design of this activity had a twofold result: First, the training initiative focused on leveraging an individual's natural behavior to sell, as well as providing the manager with skills to coach. Second, these same individuals could in turn use the newly acquired skills to build optimal relationships with their customers. "We've absolutely seen the benefit of this," says Thorne. "After the first month, the revenue performance differential between our test group and the general staff increased by 40 percent."

Thorne says that Yankee Candle has been highly supportive of the new sales training program. "Our training provider's methodology allows us to understand how different people think, learn, and perform.

For example, a sales rep with a different personality from their manager might not connect with them easily. But if the manager understands how the rep makes decisions and receives information, this unlocks tremendous potential for better communications and, ultimately, better business results. The same exact methodology is then extended to individual customers."

In terms of maintaining the early momentum and success of the deployment, Exford stresses, "The success factor for us was being able to harness tremendous support by senior leadership. If you can't accomplish that upfront, you're wasting a lot of time, energy, and resources. The same goes for reinforcement of the training; it's essential to your success and requires long-term support by internal champions."

6

The Science of Sales Coaching

Managers have to be many things to their employees: coach, mentor, even friend. If you're going to be effective, you need to get into the world of the employee. If I stay in the world of "who I am" you can't really understand where other people are coming from. Assessments give you a better understanding of the individual traits and common traits that your employees bring to the table. That's a huge advantage for managers who want to be more effective.
— David Lahey, President, Predictive Success

As we saw in the previous chapter, scientific sales training increases the strengths and shores up the weaknesses of the sales group, based upon the skills required to address a target market. Scientific sales coaching does the same thing, but at the individual level. Building upon the more generic concepts and skills taught in the sales training program, coaching provides one-on-one reinforcement of the behaviors that are most likely to result in sales success for that individual.

Assessment tools offer a scientifically proven way to better match individuals to sales jobs and career paths, and to use sales training and coaching to improve overall sales performance. This, in turn, creates a sales environment where personnel are more satisfied, thereby reducing the turnover of valuable sales personnel.

There are two general areas where science plays a role in sales coaching. First, behavioral assessment provides insight into the personality of both the sales manager and the sales rep, allowing the manager to better understand his management style and the motivational needs of the sales rep. Second, skills assessment allows the sales managers to understand exactly what skill area needs improvement and how to coach the rep for increased sales performance and long-term change.

Sales Coaching and Behavioral Assessment

One of the most difficult challenges that any manager faces is helping an employee to improve performance. This process of coaching is particularly important in sales environments, because the nature of the work requires constant improvement and honing of sales skills.

In theory, sales coaching means helping people to learn and integrate sales skills that will allow them to achieve higher levels of sales success. In practice, however, sales coaching is often haphazard and ineffective, primarily because it is seldom subjected to any kind of scientific measurement.

For example, some sales managers believe that they're providing coaching simply by evaluating, and reporting on, a sales reps performance. This usually takes the form of a quarterly or yearly review, where the sales manager provides a debriefing of what the sales rep is doing right and wrong.

Such coaching, however, is unlikely to change or reinforce employee behavior for several reasons. First, these evaluations take place at regular intervals that have nothing to do with the individual needs of the sales rep. Second, evaluations tend to focus on what happened in the past rather than what needs to change in the future. Finally, evaluations are all about paychecks, paperwork, and bureaucracy, none of which have much relevance to day-to-day behavior and developing better sales skills.

Even sales managers who understand that sales coaching is different from an employee evaluation often avoid it. Some, for example, believe that they're too busy to coach. After all, with duties ranging from reporting to top management, handling problem customers, interfacing with marketing and filling out those pesky employee evaluations, many sales managers feel swamped. As a result, they treat coaching as something that's to be fitted into whatever time remains.

Other sales managers avoid coaching because they don't like giving feedback, especially to sales reps who may have more experience than the managers themselves. In many cases, sales reps don't seem to appreciate the help, and may react negatively to what they see as criticism.

Another sore spot is when sales managers who were once top sales performers go on a sales call with a rep and then coach by demonstrating how it's done. While some sales reps may find this learn by watching method useful, others find it intrusive and irritating.

All of these problems are the result of a lack of fundamental information on the motivational needs of the rep. The sales manager has her own idea of how people learn, based upon how she learns, and colored by her own personal needs and desires. At the same time, the sales rep may have very different motivational needs and requirements in order to be effectively coached. This is important because, if a manager provides feedback or coaching that plays into the wrong motivation, it can cause low morale and a negative attitude.

The foundation of good coaching is a manager understanding the skill strengths and weaknesses of a rep (knowing skills) and motivational needs (doing skills). When the manager is aware of exactly what the rep needs to know on the skills side and then how that rep is likely to execute on new knowledge, the coaching role is one of bridging the knowing-doing gap with ease.

Behavioral assessment provides the data necessary for managers to recognize and understand the skills and motivational needs of the individual. Armed with this concrete data, a manager's coaching time increases in efficiency and effectiveness.

To understand how behavior assessment changes the nature of the coaching relationship, let's look outside the world of sales for a moment, and study how coaching takes place in the upper echelon of the sports world.

Unlike sales coaching, where the application of science is relatively new, sports coaching has been scientific for decades. Top coaches for professional and Olympic sports teams apply physics, computer graphics, motion studies, and precise metrics to examine and measure the component parts of athletic performance, and then make tiny changes that cumulatively result in a competitive advantage.

Even so, the effectiveness of that coaching is highly dependent upon the ability of the athlete to understand his or her mental processes. For example, Andrew Godbout is a speed skater who's come very close to competing at the Olympic level.

Godbout began his Olympic bid a few years ago. He had competed in speed skating at the provincial level, but was still seven years away from being able to compete in the Olympics. Over time, he worked with multiple coaches and doctors, building himself up physically so that he possessed the physical attributes that would make him a possible Olympic competitor.

However, while his skating results were strong on the national stage, he still wasn't at the level he needed to be to compete internationally. High sport experts say that competing at a high level is 90 percent mental and 10 percent physical, according to Godbout. "Before I got into high performance speed skating, I didn't really understand exactly what this meant," he explains. "I thought the statement was an exaggeration to emphasize the importance of mental toughness in the competition arena."[1]

However, after four years of training full-time as a speed skater, he began to realize that there was more to the mental training aspect of competing than he had originally thought. However, while he had been exposed to multiple ways of measuring physical training scientifically, he needed a way to measure his mental capabilities to compete.

He therefore looked around to find some way to apply to mental training the same principles that he found in the physical side of sports coaching. He noticed that there were definite eerie similarities between the cutthroat business world and the sporting environment. This observation led him to investigate PI Worldwide and incorporate the PI into his mental training regimen.

"I worked with David Lahey, the president of Predictive Success, using their personality assessment tools in the year leading up to the Olympic trials [and] was immediately convinced of the merits of the Predictive Index," Godbout explains.

The advantage of the PI approach was that it provided a way for Andrew to better understand his mental strengths and weaknesses. Then, working with Lahey, Godbout devised ways to take advantage of the strengths and ameliorate the weaknesses. This process, of course, is very similar to the process that must take place for sales training to be effective.

Godbout was especially interested in the ways he would react in high stress situations, specifically those key moments during an important race. Using the PI as a guide, Godbout was able to develop a strategy to bring into his races, especially when it came to the ability to manage his use of energy. "Being too aggressive in a long race can be problematic, and was something I wanted to address," Godbout explains. "David

---

[1]Erskine, Bruce. "A better shot." *Chronicle Herald* 19 Nov 2009.

and I developed a racing strategy to help me remain calm, cool, and collected for a race."

For example, one adjustment that Godbout made to his racing routine was to refrain from watching races leading up to his race. A little reconnaissance before the Olympic trials allowed him to identify a place just outside of the racing action where he could go and focus without any distractions.

"Removing myself from the competition arena leading up to my race keeps my aggression in check and allows me to apply my analytical skills on my own skating," Godbout explains. "Staying too close to the racing action I was prone to being distracted and excited about the other races, watching them and determining what those racers were doing well or poorly."

As a result of this simple change in behavior, Godbout was better able to "enter the zone" prior to his race, thereby allowing him to carry a high level of focus into his own race and execute his race plan without being distracted by the races of other skaters.

While Godbout's Olympic bid was unsuccessful, he raced well and the improvements he made in his skating career have been, in his words, "quite remarkable." He plans to continue to skate and thus continue to use the strategies he has developed as he pursues his post-sports career.

What's important about this example is the way that self-awareness—a byproduct of behavior assessment—helps the individual create a strategy for more effectively being coached and more effectively executing the skills that are coached. This approach is effective regardless of the specific skills being taught.

Godbout's experience also touched on another major challenge that sales managers face: hiring and retaining people who have the basic attitude and psychological strengths required to be successful in that particular selling environment. That decision-making role is similar, of course, to the role that sports coaches fulfill when they're building a team.

A top sports coach will often examine and measure different aspects of a player's performance before recruiting that player, and then use further testing and measurement to put that player in a role where he or she can be most successful. For example, a coach for the NBA might recruit somebody who played power forward in high school and then conclude, after carefully observing his play, that he'd be more successful as a small forward.

Sales Coaching and Skills Assessment

Just as behavioral assessment can help an athlete and coach achieve a more effective regimen, it can also provide the basis for a more effective coaching relationship between the sales manager and the sales rep. Armed with the insight from an assessment tool like the PI, these two individuals can better understand each other and agree upon the most effective style of coaching.

Of course, in the case of sales, the skills that are taught are much different than those taught to athletes. However, just as sports coaches have other scientific tools to help measure and improve athletic performance, sales managers can use skills assessment tools to measure and improve sales results.

Most managers assume that their top producers will ace a sales assessment and those struggling won't do too well. However, the data often proves otherwise, because while current sales results do measure sales volume, they do not measure sales skills. It's entirely possible for an inept salesperson to have a run of luck and close business in spite of himself or herself. It's also possible for a salesperson who has the right skills to stop using them, and not be aware that they're now behaving differently.

Measuring sales skills allows sales managers to understand what's going on, in terms of actual behavior in the field, and then map it in different ways to the business results. When this

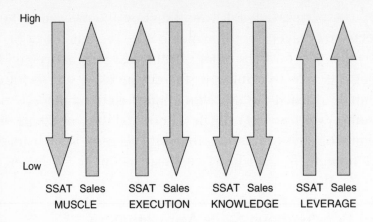

FIGURE **6.1** SSAT Diagnostic Tool: Sales Volume Relationship

is accomplished, there are four key combinations that emerge, as shown in the diagram in Figure 6.1.

These relationships are absolutely essential to understanding scientific measurement and the tuning of sales training, so we'll go through each of them separately.

THE MUSCLE SCENARIO

The first set of arrows represents a situation where the SSAT results are low but actual sales results high. This is typical of a top producer who is highly reliant on one key sales skill. For example, this person may be a very strong closer or (alternatively) extremely good at building rapport. Individuals that fall into this category are often long-term veterans with terrific results because they know their products inside out and crank out the numbers, even though their core sales skills are not actually very strong.

In this scenario, the rep is typically working much harder than necessary to get the level of results, because the rep is so heavily reliant on one skill set or "muscle" to compensate for weaknesses in another. For example, a strong closer might need a huge pipeline because a large percentage of opportunities fail in the early stages because the closer is failing to develop rapport.

In this scenario, the goal of training for this person is to build the surrounding muscles, thereby increasing sales without expending more muscle in the area of strength. By the way, this scenario is the most frightening for the sales managers who are naturally reluctant to "mess with success." Sales managers worry that if this top producer learns new skills, he or she might do worse.

However, that seldom proves to be the case. In most cases, those top producers are more than willing to learn new skills that can help them continue to grow their sales, without increasing the number of hours they spend selling, which is the only way to muscle a higher number.

THE EXECUTION SCENARIO

The second set of arrows represents the situation where a rep scores very high on the SSAT but still has lackluster sales results. What this usually means is that the rep has what might be called a "knowing-doing gap." The rep knows what to do from a skills and judgment point of view but is not executing properly on that knowledge.

The inability to execute (despite understanding what to do) may come from a lack of confidence, inexperience, laziness, or bad habits. In some situations like this, receiving the SSAT results and attending relevant sales training can be like a dose of medicine to give this person the confidence to execute on what they now realize they know, or to take that knowledge more seriously.

In this scenario, it's often helpful to take a look at the rep's PI behavioral assessment to examine if this rep is actually well suited for this kind of sales environment. Sadly, there are many bright people in this world who understand sales but do not have the fortitude to put the skills into action. In this case, the job in question just might not be a good fit.

THE KNOWLEDGE SCENARIO

The third set of arrows represents the situation where both the SSAT and sales results are low. In this case, the rep in question does not have the necessary skills and (not surprising) is therefore failing to get good sales results.

This situation is especially frustrating (for the manager and rep alike) when the PI behavioral assessment showed that the candidate possessed the basic personality for the job. One way to think about this scenario is that the person is like a rocket with no aiming mechanism. They have all the drive needed for the position but without the appropriate skills to direct that energy, they are not going to get the desired results.

Fortunately, this scenario is the easiest to solve, because the issue is simply to get the knowledge into the hands of the rep through sales training, and then follow-on coaching to confirm and reinforce the use of that knowledge.

THE LEVERAGE SCENARIO

The fourth set of arrows is the situation where the SSAT and sales results are both high. While that's always a good thing, it also presents a unique challenge when you're trying to increase sales results.

This combination most frequently occurs when top producing reps emulate the sales skills that can make them more successful. They know their stuff, they execute well, and they get outstanding results. No problem, right?

Well, not exactly. There are two challenges with this type of rep. The first is that they have a tendency to plateau, ending up with no more time in the day and therefore no easy way to increase sales. The second challenge is both more insidious and dangerous: boredom. Unfortunately, when sales skills and results are high, sales reps can end up with a "fish in a barrel" attitude that makes further improvement difficult.

The plateau challenge is best addressed by leveraging the reps' talents and giving these reps more selling time, by adding a part-time assistant once they reach a certain level, offloading administrative work, or providing more technology to increase their efficiency.

Boredom is a bit more difficult to address. The key here is to provide ongoing training and coaching that will not only reinforce what they know, but challenge them to keep growing their skills. This approach also provides an opportunity to tap into their knowledge and share best practices with the rest of the team.

Example of Scientific Coaching Taking three key measurements—sales skills, motivational needs, and actual sales results—provides the sales manager with data that makes it possible to coach with better accuracy.

To illustrate how this works, Figure 6.2 shows a profile report from an actual sales rep inside a Fortune 100 company (the name has been changed, but the report is otherwise valid).

This report provides several important insights. From the sales results bar graph, it's clear that "Stephan" has been producing fine with a solid upswing from August to September.

The table at the top of the report shows Stephan's SSAT data compared with the seven reps in the local region (North America) and all 26 participants in the survey. Stephan has above average skills on the back half of the sale process, with good scores in (1) presenting the value of products and services, (2) gaining agreement, and (3) positioning for long-term clients.

However, the data also shows that Stephan is weaker on the front half of the sale process, with an opportunity to increase his skills in (1) the opening and building trust, and (2) creating credibility by asking strategic questions. The SSAT thus tells both Stephan and his manager what skills will require coaching in order to continue his solid sales growth.

The PI data on the left shows that Stephan is motivated by interacting with other people, prefers variety in his work,

	Total Hdct	Open	Investigate	Present	Confirm	Position	Total %
Stephan	1	2.0	2.0	4.0	4.0	4.0	64.0
North America	7	3.3	3.4	4.0	3.6	3.1	69.7
All Paticipant Summary	26	3.5	2.8	3.7	2.7	3.2	63.8

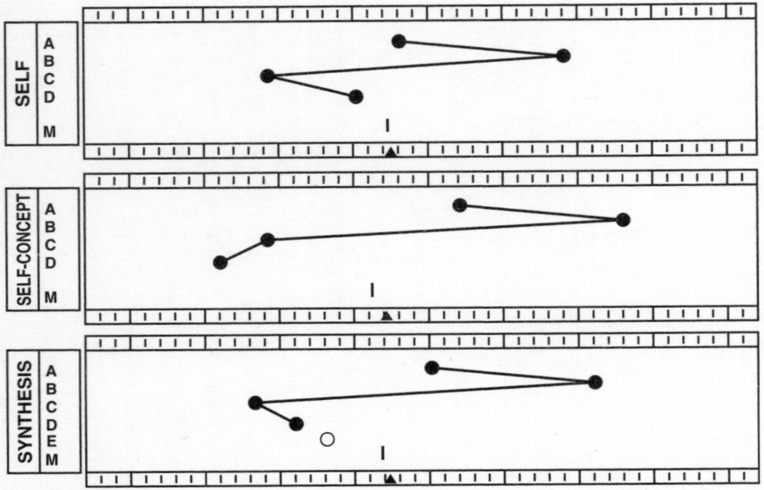

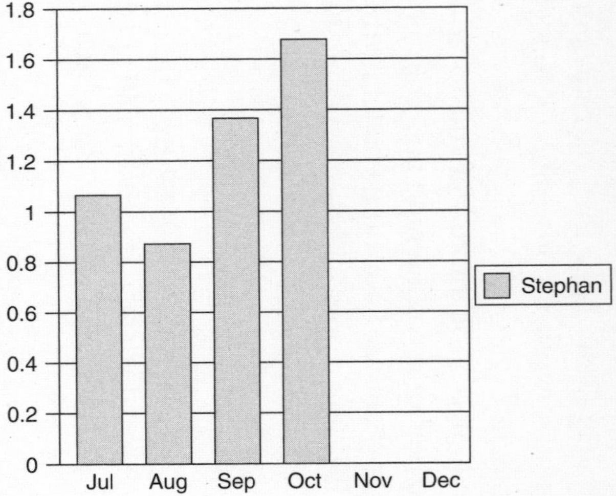

FIGURE 6.2   SSAT, PI, and Actual Sales Results Analysis Dashboard

wants to reach his goals, but also enjoys being part of a team. He has the ability to follow rules and process, but prefers some ability to be flexible and adaptable.

What emerges is a road map of where Stephan needs coaching and how best to accomplish that. For example, a sales manager armed with this data might approach Stephan as follows:

> *"Stephan, your SSAT data shows an opportunity to increase your questioning skills, by doing so you will be more efficient, leverage your strong presentation and closing skills, close more business, and increase customer satisfaction—shall we get started?"*

Starting the coaching by listing everything that tends to motivate Stephan is more likely to create a situation where he will *want* to try something new. Once Stephan is on board it should be easy to coach the specific skills that will allow him to continue to improve performance.

In other words, with *analytics* you know what skill to coach, how to coach leveraging motivation, and then (through continued measurement) you can see the impact in the actual sales results.

Contrast this with a more traditional approach that uses management intuition rather than science. In this case, a manager who knows that Stephan is weak in questioning skills might ask him to check in daily, memorize a batch of questions, and then report each night on how the questions worked. Such an approach might work with somebody else but, given Stephan's PI, it's highly likely he'd find it annoying or demotivating.

Cross-Cultural Aspects of Sales Coaching

Coaching also has a cultural dimension, in the sense that different cultures in different geographies require different approaches to bringing people up to speed.

For example, India has a sales culture that has traditionally been very relationship-based and thus very much into the "art" of selling. The typical Indian company probably worries far more about long-term customer relationships, on a day-to-day basis, than the typical U.S.-based firm. This sensitivity not only influences average scores in skills assessments, but also forces coaching to be more relationship-centric.

As India's business landscape becomes more competitive, the companies there are turning to sales training and tools to gain an added advantage. To stay ahead of the game, Indian companies want to understand the individual selling strengths and weaknesses of their sales reps, then strategically determine how best to design a targeted training program emphasizing those strengths, developing areas of growth, and providing managers with the ability to directly measure ROI.

While the rest of the world contends with the economic slowdown, India's economy has continued to grow. As a result, major industries needing sales training include pharmaceuticals, automotive, retail, finance, and insurance.

Across sectors, the increased participation of Indian companies in a worldwide market are creating major challenges, particularly growing competition, a gap between skills needed and skills available in the workforce, and a high attrition rate among trained sales professionals.

Retail alone counts for 10 percent of India's GDP and is expected to grow at a rate of 25 percent annually, yet the industry is currently working with a huge but less qualified workforce.

Similarly, in pharmaceuticals, the attrition level is an astronomical 30 to 40 percent, and the figures for sales management are high as well: as much as 8 to 10 percent.

In order to address the demands and challenges of today's environment with ongoing sales training investments that deliver data, speed, and results, the author has noticed sales managers asking three key questions:

1. How can I get concrete data to tell me exactly where each of my reps stand?
2. How do I provide training that can be immediately applicable to performance?
3. How can I better manage my sales team to drive results?

This shift in focus toward a more scientific model is amazing, considering the background of India's relationship-based sales culture. They're finding out that they can't just schmooze their way to success but instead must measure and coach more scientifically.

The need to make sales training effective (and cost-effective) is particularly pronounced in India because the country faces a 20 percent gap between the demand for sales leadership and the skills of the current talent pool.

Sales managers are the number one leverage point an organization has to turn the insight and value of assessments and sales training into actual sales results. Companies are quickly learning how critical it is to equip sales managers with more effective coaching skills.

The reinforcement, relationship building, and coaching a sales rep receives from their manager may be the number one competitive edge a sales organization has for attracting and retaining top talent, which translates directly into better performance and stronger sales results.

Companies in a rapidly changing and expanding market like India's are now *demanding* effective training, the kind providing the sales force with learning that makes an immediate impact on improved performance.

Needless to say, this is creating a market for sales training that is relevant, contemporary, and builds upon the reps' existing knowledge base and experience. And that's why many Indian companies are turning to psychological assessments like the PI and the SSAT.

Sales managers in India are rapidly incorporating the key idea that sales productivity in a global environment requires a sales team to first understand the individual and collective strengths or weaknesses of the sales organization and then the ability to customize that training to the exact needs of the group.

In India, sales managers are looking for concrete data enabling them to know exactly where their reps stand. The old saying "Hire for drive, teach skills," is absolutely true, and sales managers need reliable information to show them where each rep stands in both areas.

As a result, many companies in India are using assessment tools like the PI and the SSAT to provide critical insight on potential ability, sales behavior, and selling skills. Armed with the right data and a benchmark of where each rep is today, sales managers can then select the kind of sales training that's most likely to pay off, and then provide the kind of accurate coaching that can result in significant performance improvement.

In a diverse business environment such as India's—where industries, customs, and training approaches change from region to region—the flexibility of data-based assessment tools to provide sales managers with customized data is a significant advantage.

With some of the world's largest sales teams, companies in India are finding tremendous value with a powerful combination of personalized assessments and sales training approaches. Such a combination is perfect for pinpointing and then addressing the team's individual and collective strengths and weaknesses.

Case Study

FIRST NONPROFIT INSURANCE COMPANY

First Nonprofit Insurance Company, based in Chicago, Illinois, provides insurance coverage for nonprofit agencies such as youth services, mental health, education, religious, and cultural groups. The company writes business in 10 states and had aggressive growth plans, but as the company continued to expand, so did its turnover.

When turnover approached 30 percent, CEO Phil Warth identified it as a critical issue. He knew the foundation of the problem was in placing people in jobs that did not support their natural behavioral style. At the same time, Lena Suizzo, Director of Human Resources, attributed low morale and poor customer service to the turnover issue.

Warth learned of the PI behavioral assessment tool survey and was impressed with its accuracy. After sharing his results with Lena, they decided that the PI could help them hire the right people to fit the culture of the company and to help place them in jobs that supported their natural work style. They consequently made the commitment to train all the managers in the use of the PI.

Shortly after the training, it became clear that behavioral assessment was also a great vehicle for the managers to understand their own behavioral drives and motivations and how their communication style impacted other employees. As a result, Warth decided to expand the program to all employees as a way to create a culture that shared a common language regarding employee behavior and job fit. It is now a company policy that all employees are trained in the PI methodology.

(continued)

(continued)

The use of behavioral assessment also provided an important insight into the recurring problem of conflict between the firm's sales and marketing groups. The sales department consisted of a group of highly extroverted people that wanted things done quickly with little attention to detail. By contrast, the marketing group had the same strong sense of urgency but more importantly needed the messaging and details to be perfect before being comfortable releasing the materials to the salespeople. Behavioral assessment "provided a nonjudgmental understanding of the behavioral styles of these individuals and departments and a newfound appreciation of their efforts," says Lena.

Since implementing this change, morale has greatly improved. The most recent employee survey showed a significant improvement in employee satisfaction scores; moving from historic highs of 9s and 10s to impressive scores of 1s and 2s (1 being the highest, 10 being the lowest). Similarly, in 2002 the average number of employee sick days taken was 6.5; today, the average number is 3.77 days, a reduction of over 40 percent, while the average turnover rate went from a high of around 30 percent to a low of 6 percent.

Case Study

LexisNexis

LexisNexis is a leading provider of information solutions to professionals in a variety of areas—legal, business, government, law enforcement, accounting, and academic. It employs some 13,000 employees in 100 countries, providing access to five billion searchable documents from more than 32,000 sources.

LexisNexis was founded in 1973 to provide the U.S. law community with legal statutes and case opinions. However, the period from the mid-1980s through the 1990s was a time of tremendous change for the legal information services industry due to the advent of the Internet. LexisNexis's management realized that to remain a leader in this industry, they needed to broaden the services they offered to their clients.

The fastest way to obtain the required expertise was through acquisition. This strategy incorporated several challenges, including the need to: identify the best information and technology resources with which to merge, build a world-class sales organization to support the new information services, and develop a process to effectively integrate the acquired staff into the expanded LexisNexis organization.

To assist with these "people" challenges, the company's executives decided to use behavioral assessment to help the organization identify the people who would best fit the LexisNexis culture during the merger and acquisition process and assist in building, training, and coaching a strong sales team.

(continued)

(*continued*)

LexisNexis subsequently acquired several content and technology companies including Matthew Bender and Martindale-Hubbell. As part of the merger process, behavioral assessment was used to benchmark the organizational culture of each company to determine the cultural fit with LexisNexis. It was also used to place people in the positions that were natural job fits, which allowed LexisNexis to better blend the organizations and forecast long-term employee retention.

As a result of the Matthew Bender acquisition, Tom Rocco became vice president of sales for the western United States. Shortly after joining LexisNexis, Rocco uncovered two related issues regarding the sales team: there were no clear hiring requirements, and high turnover was having a significant impact on productivity.

Rocco knew that as the business continued to evolve and product offerings grew, the desired selling skills of his team would need to make corresponding changes. LexisNexis would no longer be selling a research product, but holistic sales solutions, and this would inevitably result in a longer, more complex sales cycle, requiring an account management approach verses an existing transactional method.

To address these challenges, Rocco needed to find a way to identify the job behaviors necessary for sales success and then match these traits to the individual strengths of his sales team. Rocco reviewed the PIs of his salespeople against the recommended PRO for the sales position. The results of this exercise revealed that the top performers were a strong match to the recommended profile while the results of the bottom performers deviated significantly from the recommended PRO.

Rocco used this insight as a foundation for establishing a hiring process for his salespeople. "It's easy to fall in love with a candidate who says the right things and has a strong track record," he explains. "What we know through experience is if their natural strengths support the job, they can do it long term and be successful."

For example, Rocco had a sales representative who was an outstanding performer and wanted to move up in the organization. Based on the company's established growth path, the next step for this person was a managerial role. The individual was promoted but could not understand why he was so desperately unhappy in the new position.

Using the information provided from behavioral assessment, Rocco was able to make the manager understand behaviorally why he was struggling in the manager role and highly successful as a sales rep. According to Rocco, behavioral assessment "takes the whole emotional part out of explaining an employee's behavioral fits and gaps in relation to their job, and in this case, why he was not performing." As a result, the individual was moved back into an individual contributor role where "he has flourished once again," says Rocco.

Rocco then expanded his use of behavioral assessment beyond hiring and job fit and into the realm of coaching. Rocco keeps the PIs of his direct reports within arm's reach to assist him in the day-to-day communication and the management of his sales team. Information provided through behavioral assessment allows Rocco and his managers to coach their direct reports on stronger communication.

The goal of this effort was to make the employees aware of their specific communication style and the impact it had

(continued)

(continued)

on the people with whom they interacted: other employees, prospects, and customers. For example, Rocco had a good employee who had a strong sense of urgency and a need for great detail. These traits were causing her to appear unfriendly, almost hostile, to the other employees.

Rocco used data from behavioral assessment to make this employee aware of her communication style and the negative impact it was having on the other employees. This enabled her to adjust her interpersonal skills to support the needs of their audience. "In this situation, it allowed me to position the actions of this employee as neither good nor bad, but more as, 'This is just how it is' [which provides a] perspective that was the foundation for effective change," says Rocco.

Behavioral assessment has made a significant difference at LexisNexis in selection and job fit along with employee communication and morale, according to Rocco. "It becomes highly effective when it becomes ingrained in the culture," he explains. "Our turnover has been reduced by 50 percent from where it was seven years ago and remains lower than the industry average, and the team communicates more effectively, resulting in higher morale throughout the entire organization."

7

The Science of Sales Management

*Everybody in the company takes the PI as does every applicant.
We've used it to understand how people on our team interface
with each other and where they're most suited to work, so that
we don't end up forcing any square pegs into round holes.
We've also created a management development program and
a mentoring program, based on the PI, in order to help our
managers become better leaders.*
                    —Ray Leathers, President and CEO, Roll Forming

I n previous chapters, we've discussed how science changes
the way that sales managers hire, train, and coach sales
professionals.

In Chapter 4, we learned that sales teams are only as effective as the people inside them and that sales managers need
individuals who can work within the organization's culture
and meet the work requirements amid a pool of applicants. We learned why it's ineffective for sales managers to
attempt to accomplish this by creating a list of requirements
for a job description and then conducting multiple interviews, and why taking a more scientific approach—behavioral
assessment—makes it easier to hire appropriate personnel with
a strong job fit.

In Chapter 5, we learned why sales training so often proves ineffective. We learned that sales training is often purchased for the wrong reasons and to address the wrong problems. We also learned that there is a more effective, more scientific approach that uses a combination of behavioral assessment and skills assessment to measure the sales organization and customize the sales training program.

In Chapter 6, we learned how sales coaching must be built atop the foundation of sales training, and how behavioral assessment and skills assessment can help sales managers better understand what motivates their employees and use that knowledge to craft sales coaching to match the needs of the individual.

However, while undeniably essential, building an effective sales team (through scientific hiring, training, and coaching) is only part of the challenge of sales management. Sales managers face other challenges that are equally daunting, and which can determine the overall effectiveness and profitability of the team. This chapter shows how a scientific approach can help sales managers effectively manage with these crucial issues.

Reducing Sales Personnel Turnover

When employees leave a company, it costs money. Turnover is expensive in the hard costs of recruiting, salary, and development, and even more expensive on the soft costs of morale, leverage, and opportunity costs. In fact, some experts estimate that the cost of turnover exceeds the yearly salary of the person who leaves, and that's for jobs (unlike sales) where a departing employee doesn't mean the potential loss of paying customers.

Turnover is a huge problem in sales organizations because, in a difficult economy, the best and brightest are in more demand and more important than ever. In addition, top sales professionals have high expectations of their leadership and expect a high level of job satisfaction. Most organizations find that there are not enough candidates to fill critical roles; a problem that's likely to become more serious now and into the future, the issue of retention is even more significant than selection.

Difficult economic times are particularly challenging when it comes to turnover. Opportunities become scarce as prospects reduce spending. Increased competition for a shrinking base of customers makes revenue harder to generate and more difficult to keep reps engaged and motivated. This can make it difficult to keep top sales employees, who are likely to look for employment in companies and industries where sales have become less scarce.

Conversely, an improving economy can also create retention problems. Employees become less concerned with job security and more concerned with advancing their careers, even if that means finding employment elsewhere. Indeed, according to a recent survey conducted by the accounting firm Deloitte LLP, fully *one-third of employed Americans* plan to look for a new job as the economy improves.

Regardless of economic conditions, sales professionals are especially likely to leave, according to Dave Stein, CEO of ES Research, a firm that measures and analyzes sales training. "Eight to ten years ago, if a salesperson worked at several companies for less than three or four years, they'd be considered unreliable," he explains. "Today, especially in fast-moving markets, salespeople are expected to have experience in multiple firms, selling to multiple industries."

To make matters worse, the employees most likely to leave are the younger workers who have the potential to be future leaders, according to a recent survey conducted by the Opinion Research Corporation. While so-called "baby boomers" (aged 45–65) may have aspired to achieve upward mobility by spending their working years being promoted up the corporate ladder at a single employer, Gen X (aged 30–45) and Gen Y (aged 18–29) members expect to change employers far more frequently.

Higher turnover rates are bad news for sales managers. Experts believe that the total cost of replacing an employee is somewhere around 150 percent of that employee's annual compensation. However, the figure is much higher for sales professionals because their departure may mean the loss of key customers, creating millions of dollars of lost revenue.

Ironically, it's often the coping mechanisms that firms put in place during a downturn that cause sales employees to leave once the economy picks up.

For example, as companies become more concerned with cash flow, sales teams suffer tighter travel budgets, slower payment of expenses and commissions, and less spending on sales training. While these actions may be necessary, they tend to alienate sales professionals, who begin feeling that the firm does not truly support their efforts. In addition, companies have a lost opportunity of equipping the reps adequately to sell in the more competitive environment.

Because of this, sales professionals often emerge from a recession feeling resentment toward their firm and its management. According to the Deloitte survey, almost half of those planning to leave their current job cite a loss of trust in their manager or employer as the primary reason they intended to look for new employment.

This is no secret in the boardroom. Once again, according to the Deloitte survey, fully two-thirds of Fortune 1000 executives understand that a lack of trust and confidence in management can contribute to an increase in job mobility.

As economic turmoil continues, sales managers must find new ways to regain the trust of their top sales performers. Needless to say, sales managers will need to move quickly to remove the organizational barriers and spending restrictions that are burdening the sales team.

The Right Job for the Right Person

Retaining the allegiance of key sales personnel will require more than patching up wounds. To ensure a low turnover, sales managers must assign individuals to jobs that better match their personality and skill set because those individuals are more likely to experience job satisfaction and thus be less likely to leave.

In the past, it was not unusual for the sales professionals to be "Jacks (and Jills) of all trades" who are responsible for everything from cold-calling to negotiating the final contract. The only concept of the separation of labor was the rudimentary split between hunters (who developed new accounts) and farmers (who maintained long-term relationships).

In recent years, however, that simplistic sales behavior model has become increasingly obsolete. Today's sales and marketing organizations are often highly specialized, with specific roles ranging from lead nurturing, to opportunity development, to inbound marketing, to field sales, to sales support, and so forth.

While all of these are sales and marketing positions, they all demand different skill sets and different personality types. For example, a sales professional who is successful at face-to-face selling may feel drained and exhausted when asked to handle incoming calls from a website. Similarly, a sales professional who loves cold-calling is likely to find working with sales technology (such as running a lead-nurturing campaign) to be boring and unchallenging. Even in cases where a rep must do it all, a personality assessment can identify the best person to fit the job.

Assigning a sales professional to a job role for which he or she is not suited almost guarantees the eventual loss of that resource.

Every time a sales manager tries to cram a "square peg in a round hole" it creates job dissatisfaction, and an understandable desire, on the part of the sales professional, to find a job somewhere else, as quickly as possible. Unfortunately, even the sales professional may not know ahead of time whether or not a particular sales job is a good fit.

Scientists have long known that individuals have measurable characteristics that determine what motivates them, and which provide the underpinning for the execution of sales skills. Through the use of a behavioral job analysis tool, sales managers can create an ideal profile for each job, and then match the characteristics of the individual on the team to that target profile.

The Importance of an Upward Career Path

It's not enough to get people into the right jobs; they also want to know where they're headed, long term. Unfortunately, many companies assume that the only upward career path for a sales professional is into sales management.

That career path, however, is not suited for every sales professional and can lead to job dissatisfaction and high turnover. Sales professionals famously tend to have a behavior profile that's entrepreneurial, which may not be suited for a management career path.

According to a recent study conducted by Paul O'Leary, PhD, of PI Europe with Ernst & Young, entrepreneurs tend to be assertive, self-confident, challenging, venturesome, independent, and competitive. They also tend to have low patience, and to be tense, restless, and driving, working with a profound sense of urgency.

That's a profile that exactly matches what's required of sales professionals inside a demanding, highly competitive market. However, it's also a personality type that may not be successful in a management role.

"A great manager has to have empathy," explains Steve Waterhouse, president of Predictive Results, a company that uses the Predictive Index, from PI Worldwide, to study employee behavior. "It's not a manager's job to make herself successful. It's to make her staff successful."

This is not to say that it's *impossible* for a top sales professional to become an effective sales manager. However, there is definitely a measurable difference in the behavioral profiles of the most successful sales professionals and the most successful sales managers.

This disparity suggests that sales managers need to customize their long-term incentives in order to accommodate differences in personality type. "A great manager figures out what motivates an employee and treats each one as if they are special and unique," says Waterhouse. In order to keep individual contributors in growth mode, this may mean delineating rep tiers to include more levels and related perks. For example, a one to three year rep starts with the normal pay scale and title; once he reaches a certain production level he earns a part-time assistant to leverage his time. By adding titles and perks based on performance metrics, the reps see upward mobility outside of becoming a sales manager.

Effective Use of Sales Technology

Sales managers are, as a rule, supportive of technologies that allow them to better track the activities of the sales force. Such technologies were originally called Sales Force Automation (SFA), but are now typically characterized as Customer Relationship Management (CRM) and (more recently, with the inclusion marketing software) as "Sales 2.0."

Regardless of the terminology employed, the main purpose of these tools from a management perspective is to measure (for example) conversion rates from step to step. Specifically, these tools allow managers to view the sales process as a discrete set of milestones. As we will see in Chapter 8, this can cause problems, because milestone-based sales processes can easily impede sales by causing sales professionals to focus primarily on themselves, their products, and how they can sell those products, rather than on managing their own behaviors in a way that will help the customer make decisions.

For example, the traditional sales process assumes that the customer needs information about your product. That assumption harkens back to the pre-Internet era, when the main value of having a sales professional work with a prospect was to present his or her specialized knowledge about products and how they could meet customer needs.

However, in today's wired-up world, the customer can not only find out about your product, and your competitor's products, but can probably find a detailed price comparison, by the time you walk from the main entrance to the prospect's office.

Similarly, the traditional sales process assumes that the sales rep's job is to sell to the customer. Customers may need to, and be willing to, pay for something in order to achieve a result, but customers hate being sold to. Sales processes that emphasize vendor-driven milestones are more likely to create sales professionals who visualize selling as something that they are doing to a customer rather than something that they are doing for a customer.

Adding technology to the mix reinforces the traditional way of looking at the sales process. This is not surprising, considering that the original application of computer technology to selling was called Sales Force Automation (SFA), a term clearly intended to imply the predictability of a modern (and even fully roboticized) assembly line.

The SFA concept, while still in use, has been largely supplanted by a softer term: Customer Relationship Management (CRM). However, the concept has remained largely the same—to apply the principles of factory automation to a sales environment. As with primitive forms of sales training, the emphasis is on making sales processes repeatable through standardization. In theory, reps are to follow a standard set of behaviors at each step of the process. The CRM/SFA system monitors those steps, much like a factory automation system monitors the steps in a manufacturing line.

On the surface, this approach seems more scientific in the sense that you can measure each step. However, while tracking stages of a sale does allow you to measure what happened, it provides no explanation or measurement of HOW and WHY such an event happened (or didn't).

In addition, the concept of a milestone-driven sales process, especially when reinforced into dogma by SFA/CRM, encourages the outworn notion that selling is simple. In fact, every sales opportunity has built-in complexity due to the nature of human beings and decision making. The old adage "process drives sales and skills drive process" gets to the root of the issue. Although the concept of defining a sales process by a series of predictable steps is helpful, there is much more to the story. The execution of each step of the process requires strong sales skills for each area.

Fundamentally, a defined sales process provides a common language and a way for a rep to understand the stages of a sale. The key to effective sales management through sales process is combining the underlying skills with the process. A sales manager should be concerned with the rep's ability to earn the right to proceed, manage the sale, and advance the sale strategically. When skills and process are combined, the rep is equipped to excel.

Not surprisingly, the failure rate of CRM implementations is surprisingly high. According to one widely cited report by the market research firm Gartner, CRM implementation has a success rate as low as 50 percent—a dismal track record, considering the time, money, and effort that is often put into making these systems work.

Fortunately, skills assessment, in addition to providing a more complete and scientific model for measuring sales performance, also provides a more effective model for creating a meaningful sales process. Skills assessment changes the focus of the sales process from simply tracking *what* happened into tracking *how* and *why* the events took place.

Building a Culture of Innovation and Entrepreneurship

Another major challenge that sales managers face is creating an organizational culture that encourages creativity.[1] Contrary to the repetitive factory-like model of selling, selling in a consultative, customer-focused way involves building solutions, finding new ways to serve the customer, and working through the various organizational issues that inevitably occur inside the sales rep's own firm.

Needless to say, a great deal has been written about encouraging creativity (albeit not usually in the context of sales). Unfortunately, much of the literature on the subject tends to be just as anecdote-driven and pseudoscientific as the literature of sales training. However, it *is* possible to use behavioral assessment to add scientific rigor to the process of creating a more creative sales team.

What Is Creative Leadership?

The University of Miami professors, Marianna Makri and Terri A. Scandura, recently studied the effects of CEO leadership on innovation, identifying new concepts in strategic leadership specifically related to high technology leadership, and operational and creative leadership. Their findings include:

- ◆ Top management talent that has both operational and creative leadership capabilities may be more effective in terms of developing streams of innovation.

---

[1]This section of the chapter is based upon two white papers, one prepared by Bob Wilson, president of ADVISA, and another by Paul O'Leary, a consultant with PI Europe. In both cases, the white papers were prepared with the assistance of Dr. Todd Harris, the Director of Research at PI Worldwide.

- While operational leaders focus on the external environment, creative leaders develop human capital—the people side of the business—and strive to create and maintain an environment favorable for new idea creation within the organization.
- The ability to create a corporate environment that fosters innovation is crucial.
- Creative leaders tend to focus on expanding the firm's existing knowledge stocks internally and they are skilled at stimulating creative staff intellectually, trusting and supporting them, and providing them latitude. They promote individual initiative while promoting integration of group activities and teamwork.

The study also found that creating a more innovative organization culture requires leaders to challenge their most basic assumptions. There are three basic rules:

Rule 1: Coach other leaders rather than lead yourself. Managers must spark the imagination of others rather than rely upon their own creativity. They must instill the pursuit of creativity into the organizational mission through informal and formal training. They must challenge the team to prioritize creativity. Finally, they must support and reward employees who step outside their comfort zones to innovate. From a sales management perspective, that means coaching reps rather than doing for them. The impact on a joint sales call is the difference between leading the sales call and having the rep lead the call; certainly the latter reinforces innovation and creativity.

Rule 2: Strengthen your ability to persuade and influence. Managers must lead by working together toward a shared vision rather than by command-and-control methods. They must relinquish some control in favor of building more mutual trust throughout the organization. Furthermore, they mustn't foist their own logic upon the thought processes of the organizations. Instead, they must discover the logic with your team, building on the team member's own perceptions. The best application for sales managers is to take the time to listen to their team members, leverage science to understand their motivations and needs, and utilize all three to increase their ability to influence their teams.

Rule 3: Use a wide range of communication approaches. Rather than depending upon traditional top-down organizational communication, managers must employ less formal channels that are more likely to encourage innovation. This means using blogs, Internet presence, instant messaging and social networking, and so forth, all of which are perceived as being credible (and often faster) than traditional top-down communication. In a world of high-tech, it's critical to balance high-tech with high touch—a sales manager has all methods of contact with reps—calls, e-mail, and social media; the key is to connect and communicate effectively.

This concept of Creative Leadership is obviously dependent on having the right people to make this a strategic initiative for the organization. It requires sales managers who are willing to instill an environment that encourages this type of thinking. The challenge, of course, is identifying these individuals and cultivating them within the organization. That's where science comes in.

How to Implement Creative Leadership

It's a truism that everyone has *some* ability to be creative. However, it is the environment in which these people operate that will either stimulate creative behavior or shut it down. It is therefore the responsibility of senior management to build an organization that encourages teamwork and team-oriented problem solving. Managers should be empowered to put employees in situations where they can generate creativity in ways where they'll be able to deliver successful results.

It's also a truism that people enjoy being creative . . . when that effort suits them. However, most people don't enjoy being asked to be creative in a way in which they are uncomfortable. For example, a naturally quiet person is likely to find a brainstorming session to be an annoying waste of time. Similarly, a results-driven extrovert might be willing to quit rather than attend a touchy-feely seminar intended to encourage out-of-the-box thinking.

Behavioral assessment helps managers identify individuals with various styles of creative potential and the rewards that are most meaningful to those various individuals. The Predictive Index, for example, measures four primary factors.

- Dominance: The degree to which an individual seeks to control his or her environment. Individuals who are highly motivated by this dimension are independent, assertive, and self-confident. Individuals who are less motivated by this dimension are agreeable, cooperative, and accommodating.
- Extroversion: The degree to which an individual seeks social interaction with other people. Individuals who are highly motivated by this dimension are outgoing, persuasive, and socially poised. Individuals who are less motivated by this dimension are serious, introspective, and task-oriented.
- Patience: The degree to which an individual seeks consistency and stability in his or her environment. Individuals who are highly motivated by this dimension are patient, consistent, and deliberate. Individuals who are less motivated by this dimension are fast-paced, urgent, and intense.

♦ Formality: The degree to which an individual seeks to conform to formal rules and structure. Individuals who are highly motivated by this dimension are organized, precise, and self-disciplined. Individuals who are less motivated by this dimension are informal, casual, and uninhibited.

There are three aspects of personality that provide the most insight into creativity—those highly motivated by dominance, less motivated by extroversion, and formality.

Highly dominant people are creative because they view their way of doing things as the preferred way. They look at what exists and ask themselves, "Is there a better way of doing this that I could conceive?" As change agents, the existing world is always better off when changed into something of their creation. Getting their self-confidence from within, high-dominance people find little that thwarts their efforts from the outside—theirs is the best way to go.

Less extroversion brings another aspect of creativity to the fore. When faced with ideas, rather than bounce those ideas off of other people as highly extroverted people do, they roll the ideas around internally in their heads—trying to figure out a solution. Less extroverted people are thinkers. Creativity, being defined as an intellectual exercise, is thus a less extroverted endeavor.

Less formality adds the third dimension to the mix, yielding in those that possess all three dimensions—highly dominant, low extroversion, and low formality—a more creative personality, because less formal people innately want to go against the grain. Where highly formal people try to follow the tried and true path, less formal people eschew all ways that have been tried previously. They want to go "Where no man has gone before ...." Low formality also adds an element of stubbornness that can be helpful to the process of creativity.

While the model is not one-size-fits-all, it's clear that understanding the PI of the individuals on a team can help a sales manager identify potentially creative people without predefining the creative process. In other words, you can use the science of behavioral assessment to establish an environment that will stimulate the creativity of the entire team.

Fostering Entrepreneurship

Entrepreneurship provides substantial benefits to individuals, corporations, and societies. It can be a driver of job creation, innovation, economic mobility, and a sense of independence and personal accomplishment. In sales organizations, entrepreneurship encourages sales reps to own the customer's problem and its solution. An entrepreneurial sales rep thinks of himself or herself as running a business whose function is to help the customer.

Over the past few years, academic disciplines such as business, economics, sociology, and psychology are all making significant contributions to our understanding of entrepreneurship. As a result, we can now apply the science of psychology to provide perspective into what conditions enable and promote venture creation. More importantly, we can map that perspective into the unique needs of a sales organization, and provide guidance for sales managers who want to foster it.

According to the research, the personal characteristics of those who view entrepreneurship as a career choice, persist at it, and succeed at it, can be distinctive. Nascent entrepreneurs are often relatively comfortable with ambiguity, uncertainty and risk, feel that they strongly and directly influence events (self-efficacy), and have high levels of work motivation.

One recent finding is that contrary to the popular conception of successful entrepreneurs being solely independent, single-minded, and devoted to their unique passions, they are also often characterized by high levels of social competence and social intelligence, with an ability to connect with others on a social and interpersonal level. Research that has recently emerged from Ireland points to some very clear personality-entrepreneurship links as measured by the PI.

In a September 2009 study of 100 finalists of the Ernst and Young Entrepreneur of the Year Program, dating back to 1998, it was found that:

- Seventy percent of Ireland's most successful entrepreneurs shared a common core personality profile as measured by the Predictive Index.
- Eighty-two percent of the entrepreneurs studied were assertive, self-confident, challenging, venturesome, independent, and competitive individuals.
- Eighty-five percent had low patience and were tense, restless, and driving individuals, who worked with a profound sense of urgency.

A very distinctive PI profile for the entrepreneurs emerged from the data. Attributes of this typical entrepreneurship profile include:

- Proactive, assertive, has a sense of urgency for achieving their goals
- Communicates directly and to the point
- Challenging of the world
- Independent in putting forth their own ideas, which are often innovative and, if implemented, cause change
- Impatient for results, they will put pressure on themselves and others for rapid implementation
- Less productive when doing routine work
- Task-focused; they often notice and are driven to fix technical problems
- Ability to work through any personal/emotional issues
- Aptitude to spot trends in data or figure out how complex systems work

- Independent in thinking and action
- Confident in taking action without input from others
- Assertive drive to accomplish their personal goals by working around or through roadblocks

These recent findings from Ireland largely replicated a 2006 study of the personality traits of 60 successful entrepreneurs drawn from France using a mature and robust empirical indicator (Predictive Index) to measure and describe personality, drives, motivational needs, and perceptions of the demands of the environment.

The 2006 study found that 65 percent of participants in the study shared a common personality profile, and 85 percent shared common perceptions of behavioral demands required for performance. The findings of this study not only represent major progress in this area of entrepreneurship research, but also have important implications for theory, future research, policy, and practice.

The insights provided by this study provide a framework for organizational development. Sales managers who want sales reps who can be (and want to be) entrepreneurial can use behavioral assessments, not just to select team members, but to actively cultivate existing ones.

Entrepreneurial performance (indeed any individual's performance in a given role) is largely a function of personality and skills. Because skills can be continually learned, developed, and honed, but character is fixed and stable, a prerequisite to top performance in any role is getting the personality-fit right. The key point is that while personality is a function of genetics and life experiences, by the end of a person's formative years character is fixed and does not change in the vast majority of people thereafter. The saying "hire for drive, teach skills" helps keep the relationship of the two in mind.

An individual, therefore, with an ideal skills-fit but a poor personality-fit for a given role will be unlikely to have the potential to be a consistent top performer because personality is fixed. On the other hand, an individual with an ideal character-fit but a poor skills-fit for a given role will have greater potential to be a consistent top performer because skills are learned.

In addition to the importance of personality, research indicates that successful entrepreneurs often seem to view the world and the potential risks in it through a different lens. For example, successful entrepreneurs may have a unique ability to see opportunities that other people fail to recognize. Or they may judge ambiguous business conditions in more positive, enthusiastic, and optimistic terms than others would.

Psychology also has a lot to tell us about the role of intelligence in entrepreneurial success. There is some evidence that general mental ability as measured by standardized assessments positively predicts some entrepreneurial outcomes, and higher levels of educational attainment typically predict self-employment.

However, perhaps another type of intelligence is even more important to the eventual success of an entrepreneurial venture. Some blend of critical analytical thinking, creativity, and practical implementation of ideas, which psychologists often refer to as successful intelligence can also predict important outcomes such as business growth rate. Entrepreneurs with higher levels of successful intelligence are likely to be better positioned to navigate the environment that they are in—an environment often characterized by urgency, uncertainty, insufficient resources, and rapid change.

Good business and sales leaders in the modern organization often possess entrepreneurial traits such as innovation, creativity, and risk taking. But just as importantly, and perhaps more so, they establish corporate cultures, sales teams, and business practices that support and nourish entrepreneurship throughout the enterprise.

This entrepreneurial mind-set may be especially important in knowledge-intensive areas and emerging markets such as financial services, consulting, biotechnology, pharmaceuticals, and a host of others. Effective sales managers not only tolerate mistakes, they actually encourage them, and they find the right balance between protecting existing revenue streams and promoting the concepts that will be critical to future success.

The Importance of Nonentrepreneurial Creativity

Needless to say, if the sales role needs a component of creativity for success, sales managers should make efforts to identify and hire people who have naturally occurring entrepreneurial traits such as independence, confidence, and comfort with risk and ambiguity, and then coach and mentor them in a way that supports those traits, such as removing burdensome bureaucratic controls.

However, it is important to note that everyone in an organization has the power to contribute to innovation, although they may approach it in different ways and need different support from their managers. For example, a team member whose natural inclination is to rely on established precedents when making decisions and to limit risk can still be creative, even though that person has tendencies that one would normally associate with entrepreneurship.

A good sales manager can help that person be more innovative by doing things such as clearly communicating that it is part of the job to be on the lookout for improvement opportunities, helping him or her to mitigate the risk when trying new things, and strongly supporting those efforts by being encouraging and by helping absorb some of the fallout when mistakes are made.

Experience says that innovation can come from anywhere, and not every new idea has to be a blockbuster. The potential for highly lucrative returns and the accompanying attention they generate often lures executives into a desire to seek the next game changer. Along the way, an enormous amount of resources can be expended, all the while in pursuit of a payoff that may be rare and unpredictable.

Companies that truly master innovation look for many incremental opportunities to be innovative, and do so not only in traditional creative areas such as new product development but across the organization in functional areas such as sales, finance, or processes such as procurement or recruiting.

Ideally, a combination of behavior assessment and skills assessment, combined with science-based training and coaching, can help a sales manager create a culture of collaboration and communication. This is important because successful innovations need multiple connections across an organization to survive, and these connections are often a mixture of formal and informal ones.

Successful innovation teams often have one or more members who are particularly adept at reaching out to other parts of the core business to find the requisite skills and resources that their projects need, and to build support for their efforts. Communication is critical as well, both with respect to articulating potentially radical, disruptive, and technically complex ideas in a way that people can understand, see the value in and be comfortable with, and also doing so in a way that fosters a sense of inclusion and interpersonal connection.

Using Science to Manage Change

One of the most difficult jobs that any manager faces is managing change, especially when that change is thrust upon the organization.

If the current series of economic crises indicate anything, it is that countless companies were unprepared for a stormy economy and, as such, they have had to cut expenses, reduce hiring, and in worst-case scenarios, lay off people. According to a recent Watson Wyatt survey, one-third of U.S. companies do not have a workforce contingency plan in place to respond to the economic crisis, and those that do, more than half are only focused on layoffs.

In difficult, changing times, sales managers must take a critical look at their staff and recession proof their company. Furthermore, they must identify who on their team they can rely upon versus those who might jump ship at the earliest sign of trouble. Unfortunately, without some form of science and assessment, sales managers are forced to make these decisions based purely upon gut feeling, internal politics, and plain blind change.

If we take anything away from this economic crisis, it is that companies must prepare for the worst even during the best of times, as things can change quickly and it is imperative that a company has a strong core of employees in place so that when the economy turns around (as it always does) the company is poised for success.

To do this, sales managers must ask (and obtain answers for) the following three questions:

1. Who is more concerned with having a rewarding job and their impact on the organization rather than financial gains?
2. Who is best suited to adapt to the changes in their work environment and succeed in a role of increased responsibility and poised to become a leader within the company?
3. Who is motivated in their current role and who is hiding their need for new challenges and responsibilities?

Managers should not rely solely on their gut feeling regarding the capabilities and mind-sets of their people based on their day-to-day observations, particularly during a tough economy when many employees can be more concerned about losing their job than voicing any discontent.

At the same time, it is important for managers to remember that even in down economies with high unemployment rates, a company's top performers always have options and may not be afraid to leave for a more appealing position with another company.

How then can sales managers engage and motivate their staff, ensuring a higher level of employee satisfaction and retention? The answer lies in the continued application of science to hiring, job assignments, training, and coaching. Here are five ways to do this:

Method 1: Use behavioral assessment to strengthen the manager/employee relationship. Studies of successful businesses indicate that the quality of employee life is largely a function of the quality of leadership. Therefore, it is vital that managers understand what motivates their employees to come to work every day and perform at 110 percent, and also recognize how their communication style directly impacts their relationship with their team and that any miscommunication requires the manager to adjust their management style, not the other way around. By identifying critical relationship patterns through behavioral assessment, managers and employees can improve compatibility and maximize productivity, especially if they find themselves in a new or changed role after a company or team has been restructured. Managers who focus on creating successful relationships will be able to assign individuals to roles where they are most likely to be motivated and productive.

Method 2: Understand and appreciate everything employees bring to the table. Assessments are a recognized way to help managers understand what naturally motivates their employees and in which environments they are most productive. In fact, nearly 40 percent of large U.S. companies use these assessments within their organizations. Once equipped with this behavioral knowledge, managers can provide the leadership to ensure their staff is fully engaged and productive. An employee will notice when his or her manager has taken an interest in their individual development and appreciate the guidance they have to offer, positioning them to succeed.

Method 3: Become more creative in how you motivate and reward your team. Every person is motivated differently and it is imperative to find out what these motivations are for your employees. By using tools such as behavioral assessments, a manager can know if their top performer would best respond to public recognition, a personal note of congratulations, additional time off, or a gift certificate for their family. Such distinctions can greatly assist a manager in ensuring that their team is being properly incentivized and strengthening their commitment to the company.

Method 4: Don't guess about your employee's happiness and satisfaction. In tough economic times many employees are understandably reluctant to make it known when they are unhappy. However, managers can be more confident in how they manage their staff if they have hard data supporting their decisions. Personality assessments, like the Predictive Index, can provide data-driven insights on the stress levels of employees, job satisfaction as well as what motivates them, and how they view their role within the company. Such data can result in a more effective and productive management style.

Method 5: Provide a clear path for advancement into leadership roles. An established leadership development program that incorporates personality assessment data helps employees understand their own communication style, ability to take risk, and how they fit into the organization's leadership goals. Companies that invest in their leaders' professional growth also help the company create a sustainable workforce with the next generation of leaders.

Case Study

Bell Mobility Canada

There are very few industries that have seen more change over the past two decades than the telecommunications industry. In particular, the advent of wireless communication has disrupted business models, generated massive innovation, and resulted in a series of seismic mergers and acquisitions.

One organization that's used scientific selling to not just weather, but to take advantage, of these dramatic changes is Bell Mobility Canada, a division of the country's largest communications company Bell Canada, which is the country's leading wireless provider, according to vice president Michael Weening.

Before joining Bell Mobility, Weening was a senior sales manager at Microsoft Canada looking for a tool to help improve team dynamics and strengthen communication. Weening first used behavior assessment with his team of 25 in Canada, then again with his UK team of over 75 professionals. The assessment process provided a valuable perspective on individual behaviors and working styles that ultimately helped strengthen team dynamics and performance and served as a team-building exercise. "I wanted to help my managers get insight into their people, and also start to understand how to build out great development plans," says Weening. "To accomplish this, people need to understand themselves and each other and [behavioral assessment] can expertly help people recognize their strengths and weaknesses and then enable them to effectively articulate their needs to their managers and build out a realistic plan for success."

After moving to Bell Mobility, Weening introduced the capabilities of behavioral assessment to his team of 775 employees. By creating job profiles and using assessment to match them, Weening and his staff are able to define the behavioral characteristics needed for success in a particular position. Then, by comparing it with an individual's profile, the company can clearly determine the fits and gaps and make decisions accordingly.

Bell Mobility relies on behavioral assessment to help managers and their staff get on the same page by leveraging insight to establish professional road maps for each employee, both new to the organization and veterans. The results are central to all discussions, including monthly one-on-one meetings and year-end reviews. This approach, Weening says, has made discussions more productive since it, "facilitates conversations that may have never happened otherwise."

At the time Weening joined the company, only 1 percent of the employees had development plans in place. Upon implementing behavioral assessment, this number grew exponentially so that today 100 percent of employees are on track to follow their individual development plans. "The use of PI has given us dramatically more insight than we had before. It is a vital tool that helps our employees achieve successes in their careers here at Bell Mobility," he says.

At the executive level, Bell Mobility has added the PI information to their formal organizational chart. Executives' behavior assessment profiles are now highlighted with their names and titles, "to help people get to know each other," Weening explains. Within the management team in particular, Weening notes, the PI has become a common vernacular.

(*continued*)

(*continued*)

Another key best practice for Bell Mobility has been its commitment to delivering targeted coaching and training programs to help the sales reps develop the skills they need to be successful. Each year, a significant portion of the budget is spent on sales training programs. The frustration with the existing programs, however, was the inability to assess or measure the level of impact these trainings were having on an individual's development and ability to grow with the company.

Weening explains (because the sales function at Bell Mobility is very multifaceted), "We have massively different behaviors within the sales organization. With such a large employee base, segmented by business focus and job function, we could not accurately make a direct correlation between a training initiative and sales numbers."

To help Bell meet this challenge to measure the skills of their sales force in a meaningful way, they use skills assessment (specifically the SSAT) to create detailed, accurate, and objective quantifications of selling abilities on an individual, team, and organizational level. This vital data has subsequently been used to drive more focused sales training initiatives, according to Weening. "When we began looking for a way to measure the skills of our sales force, we found many tools that were very complex to implement," he says "The SSAT, like the PI, provided powerful insight about how a salesperson's behavior impacts their performance in an easy to deliver format."

After Bell Mobility administered the SSAT to the entire sales force, the results created a detailed performance benchmark for each employee that honed in on their individual strengths and areas for improvement. Then, the employees participated in training targeting those areas identified for improvement. While the SSAT results varied, they did reveal a common need across sales teams for additional training in negotiation and presentation skills. "We found the results to be quite accurate and informative with scores closely correlating to the size of the reps' markets and varying region to region," Weening explains.

This ability to pinpoint the differences in skill levels had a dramatic impact on Bell's approach to subsequent training programs. "We learned that you can't take a one-size-fits-all approach to improving sales performance," says Weening. "Based on the SSAT data, we were able to segment our subsequent training to make sure we were delivering the right training to the right places in the right ways."

The results of the skills assessment also identified a group of individuals who all scored exceptionally high. These individuals clearly had very different strengths and challenges that needed to be addressed differently. This discovery prompted the creation of an elite program aimed to recognize and reward individuals who perform strongly in the field and earn high scores. This group, currently composed of 25 salespeople, receives a separate budget to invest in training programs that they deem appropriate for their development.

Six months later, the reps completed retests to measure the effectiveness of the sales training in action. Weening cites an aggregate score increase of 6 percent, which translated into significant business results. The company had "strong growth" in 2010 that continues through 2011. "The SSAT is a strong contributor to this success and it has become part of our cultural change," says Weening.

In fact, Weening forecasts significant cost savings for the company's training initiatives going forward. "In terms

(continued)

(continued)

of training programs, we had always received guidance in selecting programs but these suggestions were not based on anything tangible." Weening continues, "Our past training was also very fragmented and product-centric with no measures in place to determine whether it was delivering value."

A scientific approach to selling has allowed Bell Mobility to acquire important data that has helped it better plan and make investment decisions for future training programs. For the salespeople, the experience was also very beneficial and motivating, according to Weening. "[It] provided a good deal of motivation for our sales teams—it gave some teeth to wanting to improve sales skills [and] now there's a quantitative measure of that sales skill improvement."

Case Study

MEADOWBROOK GOLF

Golf Ventures West, a division of Meadowbrook Golf, provides turf maintenance to golf courses, cities, municipalities, and school districts. They provide products that range from a $200 string trimmer to a high-end $70,000 lawnmower. They also sell turf, chemicals, fertilizers, grass seed, and even lawn ornaments. According to company president Mike Eastwood, "The biggest challenge is finding the right staff. We're a relationship business where bonding with the customer is as important, or more important than knowing the product."

Originally, Golf Ventures West conducted most of its hiring by a combination of word-of-mouth and classified advertising. They'd end up with a pile of résumés that were marginally useful for filtering candidates. For example, there was no way to tell whether or not the person in the résumé wrote the résumé or had it professionally written. "It was a guessing game," says Eastwood. "The person might look good on paper, but we'd hire them without knowing who they really were or whether they could be successful in this environment."

Golf Ventures West developed a job model for each position in the company, so that they'd know ahead of time the profile of a salesperson, as compared to a mechanic, as compared to a person who answers the telephone. They posted jobs based upon the profiles, and when the résumés came in, they narrowed them down to eight to fifteen candidates who fit the profile. "[We use] the job profile to confirm whether or not the information in the résumé

(continued)

(*continued*)

actually expresses that person's potential," says Eastwood. "As we're interviewing we can look to see how closely they match what's needed."

Eastwood credits this process with saving the company "hundreds of thousands of dollars." He believes that inappropriate hiring, in the past, resulted in the loss of important customers, with a subsequent loss of market share. "It takes five years to win a customer and five minutes to lose one," he says. "I need to have the right people that are going to keep the customers that they have *and* grow the business."

The company also uses skills assessment to help design and implement sales training, building upon the insight provided by behavioral assessment. According to Eastwood, GVW had some of the best talent in the industry, long-time clients, and very low turnover. While it all seemed ideal, business conditions demanded that Eastwood's team generate additional revenue. As thousands of sales managers have in the past, Eastwood hopes to find sales training that will help his organization grow sales revenue.

In order to explore the concept further, Eastwood, along with his senior management team, took the SSAT assessment, which identified their strengths and areas for development. Next, the sales team was given the SSAT, where the overall scores were in the mid-to-low range. This was interesting, because Eastwood's general managers scored in the mid- to high-range, a fact that Eastwood attributed to their experience in the industry.

Eastwood quickly realized that despite the high-level experience of his sales management, that experience wasn't being transferred effectively to the sales team. While the sales team did have some sales skills, four out of five did not know how to sell effectively in his environment.

The results of the SSAT showed that the majority of the salespeople were not asking enough investigative questions when speaking with their clients, even though that questioning process was an integral part of creating a customized solution that GVW could provide. The realization that there were shortcomings in specific skills areas represented a huge breakthrough in diagnosing the organization's challenges, according to Eastwood.

Using the information from the SSAT, Eastwood and his team worked with PI Worldwide to create a customized sales training program that focused on developing their investigative selling skills. Because little or no time was wasted on elements of the sales process that the team had already mastered, the sales teams were better able to incorporate the required changes in their day-to-day sales behavior.

"The workshop [paid for itself] in less than two weeks," claims Eastwood. He cites the example of a "senior and successful salesperson [who] closed a $40,000 deal with a customer that had only purchased from our competitor for the last 10 years. This salesperson has continued to significantly increase his revenue over the previous year."

In another instance, Eastwood had a salesperson who was underperforming but knew he had the potential to be successful. This salesperson went through customized training and was moved to a new territory. This salesperson subsequently sold more in four months in his new territory than in a year in his original area.

8

The Science of Sales Process

Use the SSAT for new hires to direct their sales training. By combining CFS with SSAT, we can identify strengths and weaknesses, and use it to focus their training. Actually, we've taken that one step further, and incorporated our internal sales process (which is based upon CFS) into our CRM system so that the entire sales team can become more process driven.

—Geoff Lepp, Sales Manager, Roll Forming

S cientific selling is scientific because it measures both the basic personality of the sales professional and the skills employed during the sales process. As we've seen in previous chapters, the main point of leverage—when it comes to increasing revenue and profit from a particular sales employee—is the development and improvement of sales skills.

While it's true that the basic concept of skills assessment is applicable to many different definitions of sales process, this book uses the SSAT as a model. The SSAT, as a measurement vehicle, is based upon the sales process known as Customer-Focused Selling (CFS), developed by the author in the 1990s. While that concept has evolved over the years, it remains an integral component of SSAT and therefore provides a more scientific perspective on sales process.

This chapter provides a brief overview of Customer-Focused Selling and how to create a more measurable and predictable sales environment.

Customer-Focused Selling

Customer-Focused Selling is about selling from the other person's perspective. While this sounds simple, it takes consistent work and strong skills to become effective at using this approach to successfully generate new business. The concepts and techniques of Customer-Focused Selling apply to every sales appointment, telephone call, meeting, presentation, and conversation throughout the entire sales process. This process might be very brief or take several months to complete, depending on the complexity of the decision.

In any selling situation, there are two different worlds in play: that of the sales professional and that of the prospects. Novice sales reps typically focus only on the world with which they are most familiar: their firm, their products, and their own emotions and perceptions. This is partly because novices are often only trained in product knowledge before they actually start selling in the field. They therefore focus on communicating that knowledge to the customer and convincing the customer to buy the product.

Novices often neglect to find out the details of the customer's problems and what the customer needs to get from the transaction. This slows the sales process, because the customer may not value the product knowledge or see how it's relevant to their own situation. By contrast, top sales performers know that the key to sales success lies in the ability to understand and work within the world of the prospect/client. This sounds reasonable, but is extremely challenging to put into practice because it is easier to focus on what is most familiar and comfortable.

Customer-Focused Selling consists of the following step-by-step process:

Stage 1: Open. This is when the sales professional builds trust and credibility. It begins when the sales professional sets up the first meeting with, or makes the first phone call to, the prospect. To do this the sales rep needs to understand the behavioral needs of the prospect, set expectations for the sales call, and understand the buyer's agenda out of the gate.

Stage 2: Investigate. This is when the sales professional identifies the motivating buying factor, which is the reason that the prospect might buy. To do this, the sales professional gathers enough information to determine the prospect's decision-making criteria, understand his or her situation accurately, and know how to position the seller's company, products, and services as the best option available to the prospect.

Stage 3: Present. This is when the sales professional applies judgment, knowledge, and business acumen to offer a workable solution. The sales professional uses what he or she has learned from the Investigate step to convey exactly how the seller's products and services make sense to the prospects, from their perspective.

Stage 4: Confirm. This is the point where the sales professional gains the prospect's agreement to buy. The sales professional asks for the business, answers the prospect's concerns, and solves any problems that would serve to block a positive decision.

Stage 5: Position. This is when the sales professional begins to build a long-term relationship with the customer (i.e., formerly just a prospect). The sales professional is not finished with the sale unless and until he or she has arranged to have a relationship that includes additional business and referrals.

The Customer-Focused Selling process can be visualized as a cycle, as shown in Figure 8.1.

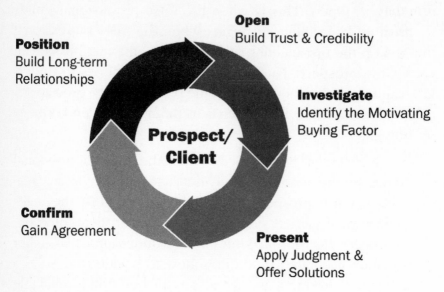

FIGURE 8.1   Customer-Focused Selling Process

As mentioned earlier, Customer-Focused Selling, as a process, maps exactly to the SSAT, thereby allowing management to specifically measure the specific skills that each individual, team, or organization possesses that allows them to successfully execute each step.

Let's look at each stage in more detail.

PROCESS STAGE 1: APPLYING THE OPEN SKILL

Beginning the process of selling to a prospect involves several factors needed to create a successful result. The sales professional must begin to build a relationship with the prospect, understand the prospect's behavioral style, set expectations for the sales call, and make an effective transition to the next step in the sales process.

All of these are trust and credibility issues. For the sale to move to the next step, the prospect must trust that the sales professional wants to help and has the prospect's interests in mind. Furthermore, the prospect must trust that the sales professional is a credible source who can actually help and is an expert with a proven track record, or at least represents a firm that has a proven track record.

Sales professionals with strong open skills (as measured in the SSAT) have the ability to create that sense of trust and credibility quickly. Top sales professionals often have a natural gift for this, but because it is a skill, it can be taught and there are a number of methods that can help sales professionals make this kind of initial connection.

Probably the most scientific approach draws upon research performed in the early twentieth century by Carl Jung, the noted Swiss psychologist. Jung observed that people had different social styles that determined how they preferred to interact with other people. This model continues to be useful in sales today as it is based on observable behavior; a rep can see how a person behaves and gain insight into what that prospect needs from him. In this research, Jung studied two key parameters about the way people communicate:

- ◆ Assertiveness—the way people put forth information
- ◆ Responsiveness—the way people take in information

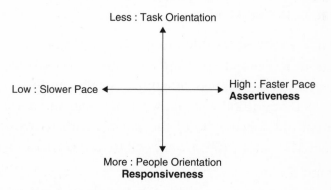

FIGURE 8.2   Social Styles Model

Individuals who displayed a tendency toward high assertiveness also tended to be faster paced in their communication and decision-making style. Those with lower assertiveness tended to be slower paced.

Individuals whose pattern was more responsive tended to show a strong orientation toward people, and those with less responsiveness tended to be oriented toward tasks more than people. Figure 8.2 encapsulates this concept.

Another way of looking at this matrix is to separate an individual into one of four categories based on whether they show high or low assertiveness and responsiveness, as shown in Figure 8.3.

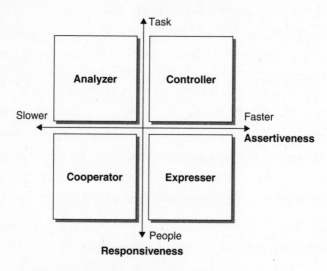

FIGURE 8.3   Social Styles Model

Each box represents a different social style that largely determines how individuals will interact with a sales professional, especially in new business situations. A sales professional with a developed open skill will be aware of visual and audible cues that reveal the social style of the person with whom they are speaking. The sales professional will then use that information to determine:

- How to get their attention (e.g., what to help them save)
- How to behave with them
- How to focus remarks and attention (e.g., what to support)
- How to help them move forward in making a decision
- What they want and need in the conversation

Understanding social styles takes time and practice, but a good way to start is to read (and as far as possible commit to memory), the four profiles shown in Figures 8.4, 8.5, 8.6, and 8.7.

The Controller	
Characteristics . . .	◆ Focused on accomplishment (results) ◆ Driving; fast-moving ◆ Makes decisions readily ◆ Clear about where they stand; forthcoming ◆ Tends to "steam roll" ◆ "My way or the highway"
Measures value by . . .	Results. The Controller considers the results generated to be the benchmark of success.
Let them save . . .	Time. Controllers move fast and don't want their time wasted as they work to achieve their intended results.
Take time to be . . .	Efficient. Don't waste their time.
Support their . . .	Conclusions since they are decisive and driven by their own options.
Give them . . .	Options. Because Controllers insist on making the decision, you need to provide them with options instead of making the decision for them.
Specialty . . .	Control. The Controller is comfortable with decision-making.
Needs . . .	Directness, speed and activity, only the detail they want, focus on the matter at hand, few pleasantries, efficient use of their time.
When under pressure . . .	Becomes "bossy" and authoritarian in order to assert their role as the person who gives the orders.
Keyword(s) . . .	Bottom Line.

FIGURE 8.4   Social Style: Controller

For example, suppose a sales professional is selling inventory control systems. He's set up meetings with two key stakeholders, a CEO and a Chief Manufacturing Office (CMO), in a prospect account. He needs to create credibility with both individuals in order to move the sale forward.

The Expresser	
Characteristics...	◆ Conceptual; big picture thinking ◆ Enthusiastic; passionate, exuberant ◆ Active; fast moving; talkative ◆ Not interested in details; trust details will be handled ◆ Lots of ideas; more than they can handle ◆ Sometimes follow-through difficult ◆ Efficiency-oriented; optimizing; finding the better way
Measures value by...	Applause. Expressers rate situations and circumstances by how much positive attention and acknowledgment they get.
Let them save...	Effort. Expressers look to find the best, most efficient way to do things.
Take time to be...	Interested. Expressers invest substantial time and energy in their thoughts and ideas and seek others to share them with.
Support their...	Ideas. Since Expressers are very invested in their concepts and thoughts, engage them in talking about their ideas.
To decide give them...	Testimonials. Expressers gain confidence that a decision is the right one when they see that others have been successful in bringing something from concept to reality.
Specialty...	Social. Expressers excel at roles requiring them to mix with people.
Needs...	Your handling of the details, enthusiasm for their ideas, reality checks, forum to share their work and plans.
When under pressure...	Attacks or becomes highly defensive. This is especially true when challenged. The defense may take the form of vehement denials.
Keyword(s)...	Big Picture

FIGURE **8.5**   Social Style: Expresser

The Cooperator	
Characteristics...	◆ Friendly; pleasant; warm; helpful; steady; open ◆ Good partner/ally; easy to work with ◆ Checks in with others; seeks consensus ◆ Sometimes suffers "buyer's remorse" ◆ Conflict-averse ◆ Sometimes need handholding and reassurance ◆ "Peace at any price" ◆ "Please don't be mad at me"
Measures value by...	Attention. Cooperators want to get acknowledgment as part of the group and not want to feel left out.
Let them save...	Relationship. When something arises, Cooperators will do anything to ensure that the relationship is not negatively affected.
Take time to be...	Agreeable. It is important to Cooperators that you be pleasant, friendly, and nice.
Support their...	Dreams. Cooperators have many aspirations that typically include others. They want to know you appreciate that.
Give them...	Guarantees. Cooperators need reassurance that they are making the right decision and are not alone in doing so.
Specialty...	Cooperation. Cooperators excel at roles that require friendliness and helpfulness or roles that bring people together.
Needs...	Your getting to get to know them; want to get to know you; pleasantness; politeness; peace; connection.
When under pressure...	Folds and gives in. Caution: when a Cooperator gives in, he or she may seek "payback" later in some unexpected form.
Keyword(s)...	Relationship.

FIGURE 8.6 Social Style: Cooperator

The Analyzer	
Characteristics...	◆ Detail- and fact-oriented; wants lots of information ◆ Does not want to make mistakes ◆ Assesses situations and thinks before responding ◆ "Analysis paralysis" ◆ Reserved style ◆ Threatened by negative feedback ◆ "Black and white thinking" ◆ Risk averse
Measures value by...	Accuracy. At the end of the day, Analyzers judge situations by whether the result or action is right or wrong and by how much.
Let them save...	Face. Because Analyzers fear making a mistake, when errors do happen they need a way to handle the embarrassment or shame.
Take time to be...	Precise. Analyzers need to know that they have all the facts they need and that the information is correct.
Support their...	Facts. Analyzers take pride in being in control of their information. It is important to acknowledge this.
Give them...	Proof. Unless you back up your statements with proof, Analyzers will not believe them or use them as a basis for a decision.
Specialty...	Technical. Because of their need for high detail, Analyzers work well in highly technical roles.
Needs...	Detail, clarity, time to think, safety, time to work on their own, written material, few pleasantries.
When under pressure...	Tends to avoid a situation. This may take the form of not answering phone calls or e-mails.
Keyword(s)...	Thinker.

FIGURE 8.7   Social Style: Analyzer

During the meet and greet section of each face-to-face meeting, he notices the pace of working and speaking for that individual and whether he is paying more attention to people or to the task at hand. He then makes an initial assessment based upon the following simple rules:

- Faster pace/Task focus is usually a Controller
- Faster pace/People focus is usually an Expresser
- Slower pace/People focus is usually a Cooperator
- Slower pace/Task focus is usually an Analyzer

The sales professional decides that the CEO is a Cooperator and therefore begins to adapt his sales approach based on the social style information of the CEO's behavioral preferences. That adaptation, of course, would be applied throughout the entire conversation and, indeed, throughout the entire sale.

However, for the purposes of brevity, we'll just examine the key moment when the sales professional turns the conversation from the social interaction at the beginning of the meeting to the actual discussion of business issues.

Another key skill in the open step is using a verbal agenda, a simple transition from the chitchat into the business at hand. There are four elements to a solid verbal agenda:

1. Permission to ask questions—this aspect gains agreement from the prospect to share information.
2. Permission to present—this aspect gains permission to share your solutions.
3. An invitation—this aspect uncovers the prospect's agenda early on.
4. Next steps—this step gains agreement to establish next steps at the conclusion of the sales call.

A very simple verbal agenda sounds like this:

"I had a chance to review your website and what I'd like to do is ask you a few questions to fully understand your current situation, tell you a bit about our company and our solutions, and then together we can look at the next steps—while I'm here is there anything in particular you'd like me to cover?"

All bases covered in a simple sentence.

Once a solid verbal agenda is established and the prospect's expectations are set, adding social style information tailors the call even more. For example, let's say during the initial conversation with the CEO (a Cooperator), the sales professional continues with the social chitchat for a bit longer than usual, perhaps discussing a picture on the CEO's desk or some awards on the walls. Then, when it seems like it's time to move forward, the sales professional delivers a verbal agenda and opens the business segment conversation as follows:

"It's my understanding, based on talking to your peers, that your industry faces some pretty difficult challenges connected with the weak economy and difficulties in controlling inventory. I'm interested in finding out exactly how you view the situation and to what extent that influences what's going on with your people and your own manufacturing facilities."

By contrast, the sales professional determines (from his clipped way of speaking and the fact that he continues to check a computer screen throughout the first minute of their conversation) that the CMO is a Controller. The sales professional therefore ends the social part of the conversation, almost immediately delivers a verbal agenda, and opens the business portion of the conversation with something like this:

"I know you're busy, so I'll be concise. My research indicates that companies like yours can often achieve a quick ROI by decreasing the amount of time that their inventory replenishes during peak manufacturing seasons. If you can answer a couple of quick questions, I can tell you whether we can save you money and how much. If not, I'll get out of your hair."

Understanding, and working with, the scientific concept of social styles enhances and strengthens the sales professional's open skill, as measured by the SSAT. More importantly, it allows the sales professional to more easily establish trust and credibility and move the sales conversation forward to the next step.

PROCESS STAGE 2: APPLYING THE INVESTIGATE SKILL

Once the sales professional has built initial rapport, trust, and credibility with the prospect using the open skill, the sales process can move to the next stage.

At this point, many sales reps launch into a discussion of who their company is, what their capabilities are, and how their products and services work. This type of approach is purely from the salesperson's world, not the prospect's world. As a result, much of the information presented is lost because it has not been communicated in a manner the prospect can grasp and make sense of in their world. This means that the effort invested will not create the desired results.

Communicating information about a company, its capabilities, products and services from the viewpoint of the prospect's world is only possible after the sales professional has gathered information about the prospect. The next step of the process is therefore to learn more and to investigate the situation. This is done through the process of strategic questioning.

The goal of asking strategic questions is to gain as much useful information as possible. Depending on the type of question you use, you gather different amounts and types of information. This information will help you to identify the prospect's/client's situation so you can better identify needs and make targeted and meaningful presentations.

When investigating customer needs, sales pros can ask three generic kinds of questions:

1. *Close-ended questions.* These have short, definite answers like "yes" or "no" or a specific bit of information. Example: "How many widgets do you use every year?" Close-ended questions can be useful, but they tend to create a lull in the conversation, forcing the sales pro to segue, often awkwardly, into the next line of inquiry. They start with "do you, can you, are you" and tend to feel like an interrogation.

2. *Open-ended questions.* These questions typically begin with one of the following words: Who, What, When, Where, Why, or How. They provide more broad-based information. However, sometimes they lead to one-word answers, which do not provide much benefit (e.g., "How are things going?" "Fine"). Some examples:

- What are you trying to accomplish with this?
- How would you like to see things improved?
- When did you first notice this?
- Why did you take that approach?

3. *Investigative questions.* This group of questions is an ideal substitute for the "why" questions, which can tend to make a prospect defensive. These typically begin with one of the following words: Explain, Share, Tell, Explore, Describe, Give, or Help me understand. They tend to yield deep information and uncover motivation, which is critical for a sales rep. They invite the customer to expound upon a situation and treat the customer as the expert and naturally lead toward a deeper conversation that can lead toward a collaborative sales opportunity. Examples:

- "Describe to me what you are hoping to see as a result of ..."
- "Explain what it is that you are looking to accomplish with ..."
- "Tell me about your goals this year ..."

Sales reps with a high level of the investigate skill (as measured in the SSAT) tend to ask more investigative questions and fewer open-ended and close-ended questions. This is because investigative questions are far more likely to reveal valuable information that will prove useful throughout the sales cycle. They also allow the prospect to guide the discussion and disclose what's important to him.

However, this is not to say that the close-ended and open-ended questions don't play a role in the investigate process.

Quite the contrary, it's useful to mix up the questions so that the conversation seems more like a conversation and less like an inquisition. Using the right question for the right purpose helps the sales rep work from strategy rather than habit.

Here are the three key rules for understanding which kind of questions to use, along with examples:

Rule 1: Start by using investigative questions to understand the motivation of the buyer.

* Explain to me what some of your primary objectives are for this year.
* Describe how this project fits with your overall company objectives.
* Tell me about your primary outcomes for this initiative.
* Tell me about the various stakeholders/audiences involved in this project.
* Help me understand your internal process on this.
* Tell me what you'd like to see the relationship with your company look like.

Rule 2: Use open-ended questions to obtain more information.

* What is important to you about this initiative?
* What would you like to see changed with the company relationship you currently have?
* What prompted your call for our meeting today?
* What do you expect from the company you choose?
* What is your timeline for getting started?

Rule 3: Use closed-ended questions to confirm information, clarify, and/or gather details.

* Have you ever embarked on a project like this before?
* Are there others who need to be involved in this discussion?
* Is there anything I've missed asking you about?

- How many widgets do you use in a typical week?
- Are you on a tight timeframe with this?

The ability to listen effectively is another key element of sales professionals with a high investigate skill level. Even if a sales professional does a great job at questioning, he or she cannot make it useful unless she is able to hear what the prospect is saying, on multiple levels. Effective listening consists largely of avoiding the following common errors shown in Figure 8.8.

Poor Listening Habit	Description
Private planning	You are thinking about what you plan to talk about next while not listening to what they are saying now.
Prejudging	You think you already know your prospect's/client's answer, so you fail to actually listen to it.
Premature dismissing	You listen only to half of what the prospect/client is saying, then jump to your own conclusion.
Selective listening	You listen only for information that matches what you think.
Private rehearsing	You are rehearsing your response over and over in your head while missing what the prospect/client is saying.

FIGURE 8.8   Poor Listening Habits

PROCESS STAGE 3: APPLYING THE PRESENT SKILL

Once the sales professional has investigated the details of the prospect's situation, he or she is ready to begin to help the prospect learn about what the sales professional has to offer. In this stage of the process, the sales professional applies the present skill.

Due to the history of sales training and its genesis in canned sales pitches, many sales training programs focus primarily on the present skill. Unfortunately, much of this training is misguided because it encourages sales professionals to present in ways that tend to slow down the sales process. There are three general ways that a sales professional can present a solution:

- *Feature/Function.* The sales pro describes the offering, what it does, and why it's a quality offering. Example: "Our widgets are manufactured locally." This is often ineffective, because customers are far more interested in their own business and their own problems and may not be able to understand how or why a given feature or function might be meaningful to them.
- *Feature/Benefit.* The sales pro describes a feature or function, but ties it to a particular benefit to the customer. Example: "Our widgets are manufactured locally, so you can be assured of an immediate supply regardless of demand." While this is better than the feature/function approach, the feature/benefit approach does not put the feature into the context of the customer's business. Even if the customer recognizes the benefit, it's not immediately apparent why that benefit is of value to the customer.
- *Value/Results.* The sales pro summarizes the value that the customer would like to achieve through the offering, and ties that value to a specific benefit of that offering. Example: "You've explained how manufacturing delays have cost your company $10 million over the past year and that those delays are the result of the inability to get widgets in a timely manner. Because our widgets are manufactured locally, we can provide them whenever you need them with less than a day's notice." This approach allows the customer to immediately visualize the positive financial impact of buying the solution.

Feature/function and feature/benefit presentations are not generally effective at moving the sales cycle forward because they both lack any concrete relevance to the specific prospect's situation. Sales professionals who use these approaches end up delivering a standard speech about the company and its capabilities without successfully convincing the prospect/client of the value of what they are offering.

In the Customer-Focused Selling process the emphasis is on value/results, where the sales professional provides a perspective on the offering based on what the prospect has said. That way, the sales professional can make targeted presentations to prospects at the right time and with the right message.

This requires significantly more preparation, customization, and an ability to think on your feet than simply presenting a canned set of PowerPoint slides. In preparing to present a solution in terms of value/results, the sales professional considers the following:

- What is the prospect's/client's motivating factor or objective?
- What is the connection between the prospect's/client's objective and what you have to offer?
- What are the prospect's/client's greatest issues or objectives?
- What is the best strategy to create a mutually satisfactory outcome?
- What does the prospect/client want to accomplish?
- What result does the prospect/client really want to accomplish?
- How well can you deliver this solution?
- What is the best way to articulate your ability to deliver this solution?
- What message will make the most impact on the prospect/client based on the issue or need you have identified?

To present a solution effectively to the prospect, the sales professional will:

- Review the information gained during the Investigate stage

- Determine the value of the solution to the prospect
- Plan how to articulate that value based on the prospect's profile
- Adjust the approach based on the social style of the prospect

PROCESS STAGE 4: USE THE CONFIRM SKILL

Most sales pros see closing the deal as the end of the sales process. From their perspective, they've worked hard by researching the customer, investigating the customer's needs, and presenting a viable solution. The sales pro is often a bit worn out by this point, and simply wants to know whether or not the customer will buy, so that they can either write up the order or move on to the next prospect.

That's ironic, because it is at this point that the customer is fully awake and aware. It's relatively easy for a customer to consider alternatives, discuss possible solutions, and sketch out the basic parameters of what might happen. However, when it comes to the point of actually making a decision, suddenly the customer's money and budget is on the line. This fact energizes the customer right at the point when the sales pro is beginning to wind down in expectation of a final decision.

Customer-Focused Selling pros see closing as a collaborative process that involves working together to ensure that the final decision to move forward makes sense. If the customer surfaces objections, a customer-focused sales pro uses further strategic questions to investigate and clarify the situation. That investigation is then reflected in a new or more detailed expression of the value of the offering to the customer.

There are four customer-focused ways to close an opportunity:

1. Time driven. "You mentioned you want to get this done by a certain time; let's look at our calendars and figure out what we need to do today to meet that deadline."

2. Process driven. "Help me understand your decision-making process on this."

3. Direct question. "It looks like we've answered all the questions. Shall we move forward with this?"

4. Direct statement. "Let's move forward on this."

The social style of the decision maker affects their decision-making style and process. Figure 8.9 recaps the ways to help the prospect/client decide.

Social Style	To decide, give them
Controller	Options. Because the Controller insists on making the decision, you need to provide them with options instead of making the decision for them.
Expresser	Testimonials. Expressers gain confidence that a decision is the right one when they see that others have been successful in bringing something from concept to reality.
Cooperator	Guarantees. Cooperators need reassurance that they are making the right decision and are not alone in doing so.
Analyzer	Proof. Analyzers need you to back up your statements with proof. Analyzers will then believe your statements and use them as a basis for a decision.

FIGURE **8.9**   Social Styles and Decision Making

Objections are an inevitable part of a sales process. Far from being obstacles, objections are actually signs that the prospect is thinking about buying. The mere fact that an objection has surfaced demonstrates that the prospect/client is considering a purchase but is not yet ready to move forward.

The job of the sales professional is to help the prospect move through this part of their own decision-making process in order to gain agreement for a positive decision. To do this, however, the sales professional must know whether the objection is actually an objection or whether it's something more serious: a condition. This is a key distinction.

Objections consist of items and elements that the sales professional can address during the sales process, such as unanswered questions, smokescreens, skepticism, and various stalling tactics. Here are some examples:

- ◆ Your price is too high.
- ◆ I am not sure I want the hassle of a change.
- ◆ I don't see the need.
- ◆ We use another company and are happy with them.

Conditions are situations that are outside of the sales process and interaction between the sales professional and the prospect that can truly inhibit the decision maker from moving forward. These include business events like corporate acquisitions, budget freezes or cuts, new management, and so forth.

Objections and conditions must be handled very differently.

With a condition, *the correct response is to position for the future, so that the prospect will be willing to buy when the condition changes*. This is very important. If a sales professional continues to sell after a valid condition has been surfaced, the sales professional loses credibility. There is no clearer way to communicate that the sales professional is only out to make a sale (and doesn't care about the prospect's real situation) than this very common error.

By contrast, objections should be viewed as requests. When there is an objection, the first reaction from the sales professional should be to clearly understand what the prospect needs at that point. To do this requires listening and interpreting, rather than simply responding.

Handling an objection effectively means identifying the request or motivation that actually lies behind the objection. To do this requires consideration of three factors:

1. The objection as the prospect articulates it
2. The hesitation in the prospect's mind that is causing the objection

3. What the prospect is really requesting in order to move ahead

Figure 8.10 identifies seven common objections, the typical hesitation or motivation behind it, and the request that the prospect is actually asking of the sales professional.

Objection	Hesitation	Request
"Price is too high"	"I don't see why this is worth it"	"I need you to better articulate the value"
"We don't need it"	"I am unsure of how this applies to us"	"I need you to better explain how this is relevant"
"It won't work for us"	"I can't see how we can make this work"	"I need you to give me proof that this solution is viable"
"I need to think about it"	"I'm afraid to make a mistake"	"I need comfort and reassurance that I'm making the right decision"
"We had a bad experience before"	"I'm concerned the same thing will happen"	"I need proof that things have improved since the last time I bought"
"Happy with current company"	"I don't see how you are any different"	"I need you to show me how you are different and better than my current supplier"
"I need to talk to . . ."	"I need to justify to my team what I'm doing"	"I need you to provide me with ammunition to sell my team on this decision"

FIGURE **8.10** Understanding Objections

Of course, those are just the most common objections and others will no doubt come up. The key concept here is that the best way to respond is dependent upon the issues behind the objection. Figure 8.11 provides an easily remembered guide.

When faced with an objection, it's the sales rep's job to put on the facilitator hat and help the buyer navigate the decision-making process. Here is a step-by-step process for handling objections:

The prospect . . .	The sales professional responds by . . .
. . . feels skeptical	. . . offering proof (testimonials, guarantees, case studies)
. . . has misunderstood	. . . offering information (in writing, descriptive, or third-party)
. . . believes there are real drawbacks	. . . going back to the prospect's original vision and understanding of the problem and solution, thereby minimizing the drawbacks
. . . believes there are real problems	. . . taking action, such as describing what has changed or will change in order to eliminate the problems

FIGURE **8.11**   How to Answer a Request

- *Step 1: Listen.* Take time to hear the prospect/client out even if you've heard the objection a thousand times. This is a key step. Veteran sales pros often find it difficult to be customer focused because they have too much experience. After selling the same product for a while, they become jaded from hearing customers repeatedly surface the same objections. Because they're focusing on their own experience of selling, veterans begin to anticipate what a customer will say before the customer says it. This slows the sales process because the customer may need to express the situation fully in order to completely understand it themselves and conclude that action must be taken in order to correct the problem.
- *Step 2: Acknowlege/Empathize.* Let them know you heard the objection by acknowledging or empathizing. For example, if presented with the objection of "your price is too high," use a simple sentence such as, "So it sounds like the price I brought to you is not what you were expecting to see?" or simply respond with "Okay." The rep needs to show he hears the prospect but not that he agrees.
- *Step 3: Ask Questions.* Use good questions (as in the investigate stage) to uncover new information about

the situation. Search for a deeper understanding of the objection, involve the prospect/client in the process, and buy yourself some time to think. In most cases, investigative questions will be the most useful. The goal is to uncover new information that helps the rep understand the objection, hesitation, and request fully.

- *Step 4: Summarize.* Encapsulate what the decision maker has said, bulleting their key concerns in order to clarify them. Obtain agreement that you understand their view accurately. At that point, they will be ready for a solution and open to listening to you.

- *Step 5: Answer the Request.* Now that the sales rep has correctly heard, identified, and summarized the request, the rep should answer it appropriately based upon the guidelines presented. Example: "You mentioned that you're uncomfortable with the investment and how this solution can drive results. Let me share some additional information that might answer both concerns at once..."

- *Step 6: Confirm Agreement.* An objection has never been handled until the prospect agrees that it has been handled. To confirm this, it is usually best to be straightforward and ask: "Does that take care of that?"

PROCESS STAGE 5: USE THE POSITION SKILL

Once the prospect has agreed to buy, and has thus become a customer or client, the next stage of the sales process is to ensure that a long-term relationship is built that can generate more business in the future and fundamentally create a client for life. The position skill is particularly important when it comes to maintaining profitability through a lower sales cost, because research has repeatedly shown that it takes less time, energy, and cost to maintain and grow an existing relationship than to create a new one.

Effective use of the position skill has the following benefits:

- Helps gain additional business and ensure new opportunities for future growth

- Maintains access to decision makers and keeps you informed and on the inside track
- Helps in the process of gaining referrals, which are the most valuable of all sales leads
- Keeps the competition from gaining a foothold in the account
- Can create a positive client reference for use as proof with other prospects

Probably the most effective way to position for a long-term relationship is to consistently deliver what's expected and agreed upon while monitoring the account for new information and customer satisfaction. A good way to make certain this happens is to apply the concept of a "PDCA cycle" from the foundations of total quality management and continuous improvement, which has four components:

1. Plan—Clarify objectives and design your plan
2. Do—Execute according to the plan
3. Check—Evaluate the execution regularly
4. Act—Learn and make changes based on your evaluation

This cycle is shown in Figure 8.12.

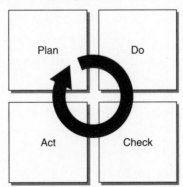

FIGURE 8.12 PDCA Cycle

This seems obvious, but few sales reps take this approach with their clients and apply it consistently. This becomes more important the longer the relationship with a client. Every business relationship develops challenges and difficulties over time.

By adopting this approach, sales professionals can quickly and easily rectify any problems and overcome any challenges in the relationship with the client.

For example, a client who's been on board for six months may be ready for a review or update sales call. The call would likely consist of a series of questions that explore quality assurance, customer satisfaction, and uncover new information. Based on the information, the rep would adjust the plan accordingly and then implement the updated plan.

The PDCA cycle creates and builds ongoing and increasing levels of trust. The Customer-Focused Selling approach allows the sales professional to consistently work from a position of strength. The relationship with the client is based on a real understanding of their needs and problems, then through the offering of the best solution. That's especially important because this trusting relationship should lead your client to feel comfortable in recommending you to others.

The proper time to ask for referrals is after a relationship has been established and the client is feeling good about their decision. In some cases, this may be immediately after the confirm stage of the sales process, but it may also come after the client has used and is delighted with the provided product and service. Obviously, the ability to get a referral several months after the point of sale is completely dependent upon the quality of the long-term relationship.

Case Study

TERMINAL SUPPLY COMPANY

For more than 40 years, Terminal Supply Company has been a trusted name in the automotive electrical industry. Founded by a husband and wife team in 1966, the family business headquartered in Troy, Michigan, has expanded to include seven branches throughout the Midwest. A key cornerstone of the company's long-term success is its people, particularly its knowledgeable and experienced sales force.

Terminal Supply Company had long used behavioral assessment to ensure strong job fit, retention, and effective coaching. When the organization learned PI Worldwide offered a sales skill assessment as well, they were intrigued and a little surprised by the results, according to Chris Imbrogno, the company's national sales manager. "I had been the top salesman for many years prior to moving into management so I didn't understand why my SSAT score was so low," he explains.

However, while Imbrogno's overall SSAT score was lower than expected, when the results were broken down, it revealed that he was achieving top sales numbers by relying solely on sheer will and determination rather than practiced skills as part of a comprehensive consultative approach.

Similarly, when Imbrogno's 50-person sales team completed the SSAT, the individual results once again seemed contradictory. "The group of sales professionals who were doing really well in our organization had some of the worst scores on the SSAT," he says. Like Imbrogno, this group of

(continued)

(*continued*)

sellers relied on a "single sales muscle" to get the job done rather than implement a sales strategy for immediate and long-term success.

Meanwhile, several people who were average sales performers or who were fairly new to the company had really high scores. This skills gap indicated the salesperson knew what to do in a sales situation but was not applying this knowledge effectively and consistently. Based on the data collected from the SSATs, Terminal Supply Company implemented a customized instructor-led training using the CFS sales process (see Chapter 8) to provide the core competencies for effective consultative selling.

Initially Imbrogno's outside sales team was not very receptive to the idea of training, though. "When you're paid 100 percent commission, anytime you're not on the road you're not making money and that really concerned a lot of people," said Imbrogno. Many seasoned sales people were also skeptical of what they perceived would be "yet another sales training program" teaching them what they already knew.

However, participants found the CFS approach offered a targeted process for improving individual skills, increasing team performance, and addressing the skill gaps identified by the skills assessment results. According to Imbrogno, one of the most effective benefits of the training was changing the way the sales reps approached a sales situation. "The key for us was focusing in on the investigative part of the consultative selling process, giving us permission to ask those probing questions that resulted in fully understanding the client's needs and allowing us to provide comprehensive solutions," he explains.

Given the fast-paced nature of Terminal Supply Company's business, many reps were not only missing new opportunities but were overlooking business that was right in front of them with existing accounts simply because they didn't stop to ask the right questions in the right way. "The investigative approach as part of the holistic CFS model provided the sales reps with a blueprint for selling into a new account or to maximize sales results from existing accounts," says Imbrogno. "The ROI on this program is immediate and is worth every cent it cost, and more."

Unlike Imbrogno's seasoned sales team, Inside Sales Manager Judy Tye oversaw a group of 10 inside sales reps, many of whom had entered the organization during a time of rapid growth and therefore had limited sales experience. Tye, who had worked in sales for Terminal Supply Company for 15 years before entering management, had enrolled her team in various sales training courses and seminars over the years but had seen mixed results.

However, using skills assessment as the basis for sales training made a significant difference because participants found it easier to apply the new learning to their own prospects and customers.

Following the CFS training, senior sales managers at Terminal Supply participated in a companion program that focused on coaching skills for sustainable results. The company also began weekly sales huddles led by Imbrogno, which enabled reps to discuss issues and reapply the learning acquired during the sales training. "These sales huddles where we apply the CFS model to address individual challenges have also increased the manager and sales rep engagement," he explains. District sales managers now

(continued)

(*continued*)

meet with sales reps more frequently—on a monthly or weekly basis—and develop a coaching relationship that "ultimately benefits the salesperson and the bottom line," says Imbrogno.

Another big change at Terminal Supply Company, as the result of a scientific approach to selling, was a de-emphasis on sales scripts. In the past, Terminal Supply Company provided support materials to help guide sales calls and, as a result, many of the reps continued executing sales routines that didn't deliver results. "The reps have been getting away from the passive approach of, 'What can I get for you today?' and securing more sales by proactively engaging the caller with investigative questions and customer-focused information," says Tye.

Within months of implementing scientific selling, Terminal Supply Company saw sales increase dramatically at the individual and team levels. Imbrogno reports: "In the first three months of implementing SSAT/CFS, we had the best month ever in the history of the company along with other milestones. Overall sales for this period were up 20 percent with a few individuals achieving upwards to a 60 percent increase."

Terminal Supply Company senior management has noted performance improvements across the board. "Typically, when we have had spikes in sales, it was usually attributed to one or two individuals securing large orders [but] what I'm seeing now is everybody doing a little bit better and taking a team approach to adding to the pot every month," says Imbrogno.

Since being trained in the summer and early fall of 2010, Terminal Supply Company experienced five consecutive months of sales increases with October 2010 being one of the strongest months in the history of the company, and November 2010 being the best November on record. For the month of December 2010, Terminal Supply Company was already $55,000 ahead of revenues compared to the previous year. The company has steadily increased revenues an average of $2 million since 2009, an unprecedented 15 percent growth rate, particularly in the midst of very difficult economic times.

Case Study

BLOOD CENTERS OF AMERICA, INC.

Selling doesn't always involve a financial transaction. Perhaps one of the most difficult kinds of sales to make is to get people to donate their time and (quite literally) part of themselves, to help other people in need. That's exactly the sales challenge that Blood Centers of America, Inc., (BCA) faces every day.

Blood Centers of America is a cooperative whose members are community blood centers located across the United States. The BCA provides 30 percent of the nation's transfusion requirements. This is a huge responsibility, so it's not surprising that BCA's management is constantly focusing on improving the operations and business activities of their blood center network.

For example, Heather Marreel is the director of recruitment for Siouxland Community Blood Bank and four other locations in the midwest region. The blood bank has 150 employees, but Heather manages a group of 20 recruiters who enlist blood donors. She also manages a telerecruitment team, and oversees fundraising, grant writing, and marketing efforts.

Not surprisingly, Heather's background, prior to joining the organization, was in sales. As a seasoned sales professional, she correctly viewed her new role as a sales position, which, until her arrival, had been viewed as a marketing function. Heather explains, "Our recruiters have to prospect for new business to achieve their annual goal and reach a certain percentage of that goal each month. We measure projection accuracy month-to-month, in the same way that sales quotas are tracked."

However, when Heather delivered the recruiter sales concept to her management team, she met with some initial pushback, but over time was able to convince the team that this was the right approach. The next critical step was a formal sales training program, and Heather's team decided on the combination of SSAT and CFS.

The initial SSAT results identified selling strengths and areas for improvement at the individual and team levels. Using this insight, the recruiters attended CFS consultative sales training, which provided knowledge and tools for improved sales performance. "The investigate and confirm components of the sales training process were the weakest areas for our organization," explains Heather.

The process unveiled an entire realm of missed opportunities in the blood bank's sales process.

For example, volunteer coordinators who assist with blood drives had never been asked probing questions, so the recruiters had only a vague idea of why they were volunteering, which (of course) made it difficult to keep them as volunteers, or to find similarly motivated individuals. Focusing on the investigate skill, by contrast, has produced a very different result. Volunteers are now sharing more information with recruiters, which has led to more volunteers as well as many new donor opportunities.

Similarly, recruiters seldom met with their clients in person, making it more difficult to build an ongoing relationship. Today, however, they now meet regularly with existing clients to help maintain the relationship and gain referrals for new business. As a result, the recruitment team has recently uncovered many new sales leads and opportunities—from leveraging speaking engagements with new service groups to increasing their visibility

(*continued*)

(*continued*)

at health fairs, symposiums, and other community-based activities.

There's also been a measurable improvement in the accuracy and predictability of their sales process. Before CFS a recruiter's monthly projection accuracy (units of blood donated per month) ranged from 70 to 85 percent. After CFS, recruiter projection accuracy increased 11 to 15 percent. According to Heather, this reflects a tremendous increase. "Since CFS, the team has a newfound confidence, and they're prospecting more and closing new business more successfully than ever before."

The PI has played an equally important role in the development of Heather's team. She shares, "Individuals are motivated and morale is higher than ever, and it's invigorating to see how well each team member works together." Heather has worked extensively to integrate all facets of the CFS training into the recruiter role to ensure long-term success. She explains, "At an individual and group level, the methods and techniques of CFS are applied to the team's operation. We conduct weekly team sessions to reinforce CFS methodology on an ongoing basis. The results have been extremely positive."

Recruiters have not only achieved consistently higher projections since the CFS training, but they have been able to sustain this improved performance. Heather explains, "Now they know the right questions to ask and how to confirm next steps to move new business forward, which has greatly improved the team's level of success."

9

How Scientific Is It?

Since the late 1980s, the academic study of personality and the application of personality theory toward the solution of key organizational challenges has undergone a marked renaissance. Interest in personality has also expanded past traditional domains such as personnel selection and hiring to touch upon diverse areas such as the influence of personality on team performance, leadership, organizational culture and climate, entrepreneurship and innovation, stress and well-being, work motivation, job satisfaction, and a host of others. Hundreds of empirical research studies, conducted in a wide variety of settings, have conclusively demonstrated the quantitative connection between personality and job performance.

—Todd Harris, Director of Research, PI Worldwide

When the concept of scientific selling is presented to sales groups, the question inevitably comes up about the scientific validity of the entire concept. This is not surprising, considering that many sales professionals have already been exposed to books or programs that use a patina of scientific language in order to create a false credibility.

The methodologies described in this book are quite different from the junk science that's become all too common in the sales training world. The purpose of this chapter is to explain the concept of scientific reliability and validity, and to show how behavioral assessment and skills assessment are measured, and why those measurements are scientifically valid.

Note: Portions of this chapter are based on documents created by Todd Harris. Those original documents (which contain further information about specific measurements and studies) are available from PI Worldwide.

What Makes Assessments Scientific

In order to be scientific, a methodology must take a logical approach to investigation, usually based on a theory, a hypothesis, or simply a basic curiosity about an object of interest. For example, we might have a theory about what motivates sales reps, or we might be curious about whether a sales rep's performance on open is more predictive of sales performance than is his or her performance on investigate. Furthermore, science must be communicable, open, and public, with publicly available validity study data, and so forth, so users can make their own independent evaluations of products and services.

Beyond this, there are four key concepts to keep in mind when assessing the scientific validity of behavioral assessments and skills assessments:

1. *Objectivity.* An assessment must employ a methodology that will not produce biased results. For example, many popular surveys in magazines and on websites rely upon self-selection, in the sense that only people who are interested in the survey are likely to respond. Because that sample is not representative of the population at large, the results have no scientific validity. Similarly, a survey that consists of leading questions is almost guaranteed to get the same responses, and is therefore not scientific.

2. *Reliability*. Reliability refers to the consistency or stability of a measure. If the concept being measured is assumed to be consistent, such as a personality trait, then the measure should yield similar results if the same person responds to it a number of times. If the concept being measured is assumed to be inconsistent, such as mood, then the measure should yield dissimilar results if the same person responds to it a number of times. There are two ways to test for reliability: comparing responses to the test over time, and comparing responses internally. We'll be discussing both of these later in this chapter.

3. *Validity*. While reliability refers to the consistency of a measure, validity refers to its accuracy. A measure is valid if it actually measures what it purports to measure. There are two ways to test for validity. The first, called *construct validity*, is when a measure is statistically compared with another measure of similar and/or different concepts. The second, called *criterion-related validity*, is when a measure is statistically compared with behaviors it claims to predict. In other words, behavioral assessment and skills assessment are valid if they mimic the results of similar tests, and if the measures correspond to actual behaviors and results.

4. *Demographics*. This element is peculiar to the social sciences and psychology. To be scientifically valid as a way of assessing a broad base of people, the assessment should not generate different responses based upon the gender, race, and age of the people being assessed, unless it is specifically designed to do so. This is important for two reasons. First, those factors are not particularly useful since test data shows that a top-performing male sales rep (for instance) will be more similar to a top-performing female than to a poorly performing male. Second, there are government regulations

that forbid the use of instruments that could lead toward a pseudoscientific bias in hiring and promotion.

As we shall see, both the PI and SSAT are scientifically based on this criteria.

The Predictive Index (PI)

The PI measures personality. While some experts define personality differently, the most common definition consists of two conceptually distinct concepts:

- *Personality as Reputation.* Used this way, the term *personality* refers to the distinctive and unique impression that one makes on others. This perspective refers to personality from the viewpoint of the observer, and is functionally equivalent to a person's reputation.
- *Personality as Identity.* Used this way, personality refers to the structures inside of a person that are useful in explaining why a person creates a particular impression on others. This is personality from the perspective of the actor, concerned with how a person perceives him- or herself, and is functionally equivalent to a person's identity.

Within that definition, the PI measures four primary and fundamental personality constructs:

1. *Dominance*: The degree to which an individual seeks to control his or her environment. Individuals who score high on this dimension are independent, assertive, and self-confident. Individuals who score low on this dimension are agreeable, cooperative, and accommodating.
2. *Extroversion*: The degree to which an individual seeks social interaction with other people. Individuals who score high on this dimension are outgoing, persuasive,

and socially poised. Individuals who score low on this dimension are serious, introspective, and task-oriented.

3. *Patience*: The degree to which an individual seeks consistency and stability in his or her environment. Individuals who score high on this dimension are patient, consistent, and deliberate. Individuals who score low on this dimension are fast-paced, urgent, and intense.

4. *Formality*: The degree to which an individual seeks to conform to formal rules and structure. Individuals who score high on this dimension are organized, precise, and self-disciplined. Individuals who score low on this dimension are informal, casual, and uninhibited.

The PI also measures two secondary personality constructs, which are derived from a combination of each of the four primary personality constructs described previously:

1. *Decision Making*: Measures how an individual processes information and makes decisions. Individuals who score high on this dimension are objective, logical, and are primarily influenced by facts and data. Individuals who score low on this dimension are subjective, intuitive, and are primarily influenced by feelings and emotions.

2. *Response Level*: Measures an individual's overall responsiveness to the environment, which is reflected in his or her energy, activity level, and stamina. Individuals who score high on this dimension have an enhanced capacity to sustain activity and tolerate stress over longer periods of time. Individuals who score low on this dimension have less of this capacity.

The scoring of the PI checklist produces a behavioral pattern with three elements, known as the self, the self-concept, and the synthesis. The self measures a person's natural, basic, and enduring personality. The self-concept measures the ways in which a person is trying to modify his or her behavior to satisfy perceived environmental demands. Lastly, the synthesis, which is a combination of the self and self-concept, measures the ways in which a person typically behaves in his or her current environment.

The PI has been in widespread commercial use since 1955, with minor revisions to the assessment occurring in 1958, 1963, 1988, and 1992. These minor revisions were undertaken to improve both the PI's psychometric properties and to ensure that each of the individual items on the assessment conformed to appropriate and contemporary language norms.

The PI is currently used by over 7,800 organizations across a wide variety of industries and company sizes, including 51 companies listed in the 2009 Fortune 500, and 82 companies listed in the 2009 Fortune Global 500. Organizations that use the PI are located in 143 different countries, with approximately 30 percent of PI utilization occurring outside of North America.

In 2010, over one million people around the world completed the PI assessment. The PI is used for a variety of talent management purposes, such as personnel selection, executive on-boarding, leadership development, succession planning, performance coaching, team building, and organizational culture change among others.

THE OBJECTIVITY OF THE PI

The PI measures the personality as identity aspect of personality, and has been developed and validated exclusively for use within occupational and organizational populations. To do this, it employs a scientific methodology similar to other psychological measurement instruments.

Specifically, the PI employs a free-choice (as opposed to forced-choice) response format, in which individuals are presented with two lists of descriptive adjectives, both containing 86 items, and are asked to endorse those that they feel describe them (the self domain), and then those that they feel coincide with how they feel others expect them to behave (the self-concept domain).

Summing across these two domains yields a third implied domain (the synthesis), which can be interpreted as reflecting an employee's observable behavior in the workplace. The assessment is not timed, generally takes approximately five to ten minutes to complete, and is available in paper-and-pencil, desktop, and Internet formats.

Such methodologies are generally considered to be scientifically objective within the fields of psychology and social science.

THE RELIABILITY OF THE PI

As mentioned earlier, reliability refers to the consistency or stability of a measure. If the concept being measured is assumed to be consistent, such as a personality trait, then the measure should yield similar results if the same person responds to it a number of times. If the concept being measured is assumed to be inconsistent, such as mood, then the measure should yield dissimilar results if the same person responds to it a number of times.

One way to estimate reliability is by computing the measure's test-retest reliability. Test-retest reliability is perhaps the easiest assessment of a measuring device's reliability to conceptualize and understand. Using the same group of people, a construct is measured at two separate points in time and then the two sets of scores are compared.

This technique yields a correlation often known as the coefficient of stability, because it reflects the stability of test scores over time. If the measure under study is reliable, people will have scores that are similar across trials. Note that the shorter the time interval between administrations of the test (e.g., two weeks versus three months), the higher will be the test-retest coefficient.

The test-retest reliability of the PI was first examined in 1983, 1999, 2009, and 2011. Taken as a whole, the results from these tests indicate that the PI demonstrates acceptable levels of test-retest reliability.

A second way to estimate reliability is by computing the measure's internal consistency reliability. This is accomplished by determining whether the individual items on the assessment intended to measure the same construct (such as dominance) are mathematically related.

Internal consistency methods estimate the reliability of a test based solely on the number of items within the test and the average intercorrelation among those items. The internal consistency reliability of the PI has been examined in three different studies. The average internal consistency reliability of PI Factors across these studies is .85, with a range of .82 to .87.

Although estimates vary, the lower boundary for the acceptability of internal consistency reliability is often taken as .70. There may also be an upper boundary of acceptability as well, perhaps .90 or above, that may signal measurement redundancy across some of the items.

THE VALIDITY OF THE PI

As previously described, validity refers to the accuracy of a measure. A measure is valid if it actually measures what it purports to measure.

Construct validity is demonstrated when a measure is statistically compared with another measure of similar and/or different concepts. To be successful, the comparison measure must have been soundly constructed and be generally accepted. Such research on the PI has been conducted twice. Both of these studies compared the PI with Raymond Cattell's 16PF. (The 16PF is a well-respected and well-researched personality assessment.)

A construct validity study involves looking at patterns of correlations. Correlations are mathematical measures that can identify the presence and strength of the relationship between two variables. A pattern should emerge that meets the following expectations: Factors that are defined in a similar way by both the PI and the 16PF should prove to be very similar statistically (e.g., the PI's extroversion factor and the 16PF's extroversion factor), and factors that are defined in a dissimilar way on both the PI and the 16PF should prove to be mathematically unrelated (e.g., the PI's extroversion factor and the 16PF's emotional stability factor).

In both of these studies, the PI successfully demonstrated construct validity: the relationships you would intuitively expect should be related were mathematically related, and the relationships you would intuitively not expect should be related were mathematically unrelated.

Criterion-related validity is demonstrated when a measure is statistically compared with behaviors it claims to predict. We say that the PI is related to, and can predict, behaviors in the workplace. Criterion-related validity studies objectively show whether these relationships exist, and if so, they show the nature of these relationships.

The PI has been investigated in nearly 500 concurrent (in which data for the predictor and criteria are collected at the same time) and predictive (in which there is some time-lapse between when the data for the predictor and criteria are collected) criterion-related validity studies since September of 1976, for a variety of jobs, in a variety of industries, in a variety of countries, and utilizing a wide range of job performance metrics, such as tenure, turnover, sales, and customer satisfaction.

This body of evidence supports the fact that the PI is indeed consistently related to important workplace outcomes, with studies typically yielding uncorrected correlations between the PI factors and individual job performance criteria in the .20 to .40 range. These correlations indicate that the PI can be an effective predictor of workplace performance.

THE DEMOGRAPHICS OF THE PI

The U.S. population is increasingly diverse, as are the populations of many other countries. As a result, personnel selection systems that rely solely or primarily on measures of cognitive ability significantly adversely affect most protected groups, especially African Americans, Native Americans, and Hispanics. White people are often hired at a disproportionately high rate when typical cognitive ability tests are the primary selection and screening tools.

These adverse impacts created substantial pressure on companies to find equally valid but less discriminatory selection techniques. Research on personality variables indicates that they have much less, and often no, adverse impact on members of protected groups,[1] a tremendous advantage when dealing with increasingly heterogeneous customer, supplier, and employee bases.

PI Worldwide has performed significant research to determine whether the PI discriminates against protected classes. In a report written by Dr. Richard Wolman of Harvard University, the PI was analyzed to determine whether men and women tended to score differently on the PI, and whether African Americans, Hispanics, and Caucasians tended to score differently on the PI. His analyses showed that neither gender nor race was significantly related to the PI scores.

In a more recent study, the PI was analyzed to determine whether the PI produces adverse impact based on age. The study showed that for all PI factors, people over age 40 (the protected class) had PI patterns that were no different than people under age 40, confirming earlier findings.

The PI has now been translated into 63 different languages, has been used globally since 1958, and is seeing strong growth in Asia and India. Over the past five years,

---

[1]Hough, L. M. (1998). "Personality at Work: Issues and Evidence." In M. Hakel (Ed.), *Beyond Multiple Choice: Evaluating Alternatives to Traditional Testing for Selection* (Hillsdale, NJ: Erlbaum), pp. 131–159.

PI Worldwide has conducted criterion-related validity studies involving employees from China, Canada, India, Britain, Spain, Portugal, Germany, Hungary, Russia, Australia, and the Netherlands. The results of these international job validity efforts demonstrate the same quantitative connections between the PI and job performance that our U.S.-based studies have shown.

The results of this body of research indicate that the PI is age-, gender- and race-neutral, and that the inclusion of a well-validated personality assessment such as the PI in a company's personnel selection system may lead to a more demographically diverse workforce. Furthermore, there is no evidence to indicate that the inclusion of the PI in a company's personnel selection system, either in a compensatory or multiple-hurdle selection model, results in adverse impact against any protected class.

The Selling Skills Assessment Tool (SSAT)

The Selling Skills Assessment Tool (SSAT) is a 25-item instrument designed to assess sales professionals' consultative and Customer-Focused Selling skills. The SSAT primarily serves as a diagnostic, benchmarking, and tracking tool that facilitates targeted training and coaching in five sales skills areas:

- *Open*: This area explores the degree to which the salesperson effectively builds trust and navigates the initial sales conversation.
- *Investigate*: This area explores the degree to which the salesperson accurately assesses the sales situation and uncovers client needs.
- *Present*: This area explores the degree to which the salesperson effectively ties his or her capabilities to the client situation.
- *Confirm*: This area explores the degree to which the salesperson effectively gains agreement and wins the business.

- ◆ *Position*: This area explores the degree to which the salesperson positions himself or herself to build long-term customers.

THE OBJECTIVITY OF THE SSAT

The SSAT is administered via a secure web-based application, typically takes between 20 and 25 minutes to complete, and is not timed. The SSAT participants respond to a series of 25 sales scenarios in which they indicate which of three feasible courses of action they would be most likely to actually take (as opposed to what they believe is the right answer). This methodology conforms to generally accepted scientific models for measuring skills.

The SSAT has been in widespread commercial use since 2001. As of January 2008, the SSAT norm group is comprised of 4,216 sales professionals, drawn from 216 different organizations, representing a wide cross section of industries, companies, and demographic characteristics. No single company accounts for more than 7.3 percent of the respondents in the norm group. The broad base of testing provides both objectivity and general applicability to a wide range of sales environments.

THE RELIABILITY OF THE SSAT

Test-retest reliability estimates for the SSAT typically exceed .80, demonstrating a significant amount of consistency for an individual sales professional completing the SSAT multiple times. It is important to note that given the types of constructs that the SSAT assesses (i.e., sales skills), which are amenable to change and improvement over time, the consistency of the SSAT scores for a given individual may vary depending on the amount and quality of sales training and coaching that he or she has been exposed to.

When we examine the internal structure of the SSAT, we see that there is a significant degree of overlap among the five sales skills areas (average bivariate correlation = .29). Respondents that scored highly in one area are relatively likely to score highly in the other areas as well (and vice versa). Additionally, each of the 25 individual items that comprise the SSAT are strongly mathematically related to the whole instrument, thus demonstrating appropriate internal consistency.

THE VALIDITY OF THE SSAT

The SSAT was tested for construct validity in an independent research project conducted by the author in partial fulfillment of the requirements for a master's degree in education at Cambridge College in Massachusetts.

In that project, which was conducted prior to her involvement with PI Worldwide, the author of this book used the SSAT methodology to create a similar test for students studying to be psychologists and counselors.

As with sales personnel, counseling students are required to master a variety of skills in order to provide effective counseling to their future clients. The core communication skills that need to be learned are a combination of rapport building, listening, and questioning, as well as others discussed in detail in the study. In addition, the core skills are combined in the more advanced processes of cognitive complexity and self-appraisal.

The study examined the skills the counseling student needs to learn, how those skills are assimilated by the student, and how the mastery of those skills are measured in the field of counseling today. It accomplished this by using a modified version of the SSAT.

The research concluded that the modified test "can provide a valuable assessment vehicle for both students and faculty, however not in its current state" and that it "could be used with additional edits to more accurately reflect both the student counselor competencies and the counseling environment."

As for criterion-related validity, PI Worldwide has conducted several studies that prove validity in the business environment. Those study results demonstrate strong correlation in three of the key areas and moderate correlation in two of the key areas.

The normative data has also been validated against specific business-related criteria such as sales results.

THE DEMOGRAPHICS OF THE SSAT

The SSAT normative data has been collected in SPSS (highest industry standard statistical software). A study completed on the SSAT in 2000 proved freedom from bias across all Equal Employment Opportunity Commission (EEOC) required fields including ethnicity, age, and sex.

The norm group possesses the following characteristics:

- *Gender*: 2,435 (57.8 percent) of participants are coded as male, 1,567 (37.2 percent) are coded as female. Gender data are not available for 214 (5.1 percent) participants.
- *Ethnicity*: 3,415 (81.0 percent) of participants are coded as White, 159 (3.8 percent) are coded as Hispanic, 71 (1.7 percent) are coded as African American, 65 (1.5 percent) are coded as Asian, 32 (0.8 percent) are coded as Native American and 147 (3.5 percent) are coded as "other." Ethnicity data are not available for 327 (7.7 percent) participants.
- *Age*: The mean age of SSAT participants is 42.4 (Median = 42.0; Standard Deviation = 10.3), with a range of 19 to 87.
- *Education*: 643 participants (15.3 percent) have a high school degree, 401 (9.5 percent) have some college experience, 1,951 (46.3 percent) are college graduates, and 635 (15.0 percent) hold an advanced degree. Education data are not available for 586 (13.9 percent) participants.
- *Total Sales Experience*: The mean number of years spent in sales for participants is 12.8 (Median = 11.0; Standard Deviation = 9.6), with a range of 0 to 60.
- *Company Sales Experience*: The mean number of years in sales at his or her present company for participants is 5.5 (Median = 3.0; Standard Deviation = 6.6), with a range of 0 to 44.

Gender, ethnicity, and age account for a trivial amount of variance in the SSAT scores. Only 2.2 percent of the variability in respondent performance on the SSAT is attributable to this group of demographic characteristics. Sales experience (both in total and with the respondent's present company) also accounts for a trivial amount of variance in the SSAT scores. Only 2.2 percent of the variability in respondent performance on the SSAT is attributable to the respondent's level of sales experience.

Studies of Behavioral Assessments

Figure 9.1 shows a brief representative sampling of the impact that behavioral assessment can have on key business outcomes:

Industry	Finding	Source
Multiple Industries	In a meta-analysis of 73 different studies, large and statistically significant correlations between personality traits and ratings of leader effectiveness were observed.	Journal of Applied Psychology, (2002), Vol. 87, No. 4, 765–780.
Manufacturing	A one standard-deviation decrease in patience translated into a $2 million difference in average sales over a 27-month period ($2,880,981 versus $554,013).	PI Worldwide Quantitative Case Study # 2004.04.01
Multiple Industries	In a meta-analysis of 163 different studies, personality traits were found to be strongly related to employee job satisfaction.	Journal of Applied Psychology, (2002), Vol. 87, No. 3, 530–541.
Health care	The degree of similarity in personality traits between a supervisor and subordinate significantly predicted the subordinate's satisfaction with the supervisor.	Journal of Applied Psychology, (2005), Vol. 90, No. 4, 749–757.

FIGURE **9.1** Impact and Business Outcomes of Behavioral Assessment

Industry	Finding	Source
Multiple Industries	The inclusion of personality variables in a selection system often has the advantage of less adverse impact on protected groups and higher validity for predicting job performance.	Roberts, B.W. & Hogan, R. (2001). Personality Psychology in the Workplace. Washington, D.C.: American Psychological Association.
Health care	Assisted living facilities with higher average levels of formality across their executive teams performed significantly better on Medicare-rating metrics.	PI Worldwide Validity Study # 11.18.2010
Agriculture	Personality traits were significantly related to ratings of overall and component managerial quality and effectiveness.	2004 Society for Industrial and Organizational Psychology Conference, Chicago, IL.
Multiple Industries	89 of the Fortune 100 use personality testing.	The *New Yorker* Magazine, September 20, 2004.
Aviation	All major airlines use personality questionnaires as part of their selection process for pilots.	Roberts, B.W. & Hogan, R. (2001). Personality Psychology in the Workplace. Washington, D.C.: American Psychological Association.
Automotive	A one standard-deviation increase in dominance translated into 46 more cars sold over a four-month period (69 versus 23).	PI Worldwide Quantitative Case Study # 2007.07.01
Multiple Industries	Legally defensible employment testing significantly reduces the risk of class-action EEOC litigation.	Sharf, J.C. & Jones, D.P. (2000). *Employment Risk Management*. San Francisco: Jossey-Bass.

FIGURE 9.1   Impact and Business Outcomes of Behavioral Assessment (*continued*)

Industry	Finding	Source
Information Technology	In a Fortune 50 IT company, 93 percent of high-potentials that received formal coaching that incorporated personality data found that experience favorable, and 95 percent believed that it would be valuable to their career development.	Fortune 50 IT company internal report.
Multiple Industries	Over 40 percent of employment decisions in the private sector are based on the results of employment tests.	Muchinsky, P.M. (2011). Psychology Applied to Work. Summerfield, N.C.: Hypergraphic Press.
U.S. Army	In a multimillion-dollar, seven-year research effort conducted by the U.S. Army Research Institute and known as "Project A," results clearly indicated that the Army could improve the prediction of overall job performance as well as components of job performance by measuring personality.	Personnel Psychology, (1990), 43, 33–354.
Multiple Industries	In a meta-analysis of 66 different studies, a strong relationship between human capital and firm performance, including profitability, profitability compared to competitors, revenue growth, net cash flow, stock market returns, sales growth, and others.	Journal of Applied Psychology, (2011), Vol. 96, No. 3, 443–456.

FIGURE 9.1 Impact and Business Outcomes of Behavioral Assessment (*continued*)

Industry	Finding	Source
Emergency Services	Personality has been shown to be a valid predictor of police officer job performance both in the U.S. and England, and the British Fire Service College uses personality assessments for both entry-level selection and career development for senior officers being trained for command positions.	Journal of Contingencies and Crisis Management, (1995), 3, 113–123.
Multiple Industries	Personality traits have found to be significant predictors of contextual work performance behaviors such as adaptability, creativity, job dedication, altruism, customer service, and others.	M.R. Barrick & A.M. Ryan (2003). Personality and Work. San Francisco, CA: Jossey-Bass.
Multiple Industries	81 percent of companies surveyed used assessments as part of their talent management process, companies judged as best-in-class (as measured by hiring manager satisfaction, percentage of employees receiving superior performance reviews, and succession-planning readiness) were even more likely to use assessments. On average, organizations using assessments saw 18 percent more of their organizational goals achieved and 15 percent more of their new hires achieving their first job performance milestone on time. Use of assessments also significantly impacted time to hire and cost per hire metrics.	Assessments 2011: Selecting and Developing for the Future. The Aberdeen Group.

FIGURE 9.1   Impact and Business Outcomes of Behavioral Assessment (*continued*)

10

The Future of Scientific Selling

There's still more to be done, more to be discovered, simply because the challenges are so great. For example, I just saw a Harvard Business Review report showing that there is a direct correlation between retention and customer satisfaction. Turns out that Best Buy did a study in which .001 percent increase in retention resulted in $100,000 revenue per store. Breakthrough results like this are only possible when you think of selling as something that can be measured and understood scientifically.
—Mike Stewart, President, The Predictive Group

The application of science to the business of selling will inevitably increase as more companies and executives understand how the application of scientific measurement can make sales teams more predictable and effective. This will be especially true within organizations that are pioneering new business models, creating new organizational models, and utilizing new sales-oriented technologies. The world continues to head in the direction of demystifying sales results and using science and proof for better analysis and business planning.

In addition, there is new research, mostly being conducted within the academic world, that will drive changes in the way that companies envision sales and the sales process. What

199

will happen over the next 10 years is the development of a feedback cycle, where changes in the business world will create a demand for more science and the increased application of science to the business world will generate further changes to the business world. The results of this cycle will continue to spill over into the sales function area along with all other areas of the company.

There are four scientific disciplines that will increase the scope of scientific selling over the next 10 years:

1. Cognitive Science—Research into how people think about and perceive information and how that experience drives buying behavior.
2. Human Analytics—Research into how and why certain people behave in different scenarios and how those differences drive selling behavior.
3. Predictive Analytics—Research into the statistics of past performance to better understand and predict future organizational performance.
4. Neuroscience—Research into the physical brain to better understand how it changes as the result of both buying and selling behavior.

It hardly needs to be said that there is some overlap between the four areas, but the previous taxonomy represents the major thrusts of the continuing effort to bring science into the world of selling. This chapter describes these areas of research, with examples of how that research is likely to be applied.

Cognitive Science

Cognitive science is the sudy of the mind and its processes. It examines what cognition is, what it does and how it works, and includes research on how information is processed (in faculties such as perception, language, memory, reasoning, and emotion), represented, and transformed in actual behaviors.

Cognitive science applied to testing an individual's cognitive ability is becoming increasingly common. Many companies are cautious around the legal exposure with cognitive testing, but this area of science adds a powerful data point to behavioral and skills assessment for predicting overall performance.

Over the next 10 years, cognitive science will play a key role in understanding the impact of technology upon buying behavior.

A prime example is the myth of the educated buyer. According to technology companies, the increase in the amount of information available to buyers (see Trend 1 in Chapter 1) has created a more educated buyer who is able to make better decisions. Some pundits (particularly those paid by the high-tech industry) have even speculated that this educated buyer is less likely to need the services of a salesperson in order to make buying decisions, thereby making sales teams obsolete.

However, for many individuals, the Internet creates a permanent state of information overload, where there is so much data available that it's next to impossible for an individual to understand its context. In cognitive science, information overload is a form of sensory overload, which can cause disorientation, a lack of responsiveness, and poor decision making.

As futurist Alvin Toffler pointed out over 40 years ago: "When the individual is plunged into a fast and irregularly changing situation, or a novelty-loaded context . . . his predictive accuracy plummets. He can no longer make the reasonably correct assessments on which rational behavior is dependent."[1]

A recent study of 1,007 sales professionals across the United States, the United Kingdom, Brazil, and China by Ogilvyone Worldwide, found that between 61 to 70 percent of sales reps feel that, while customers may be obtaining *more* information

---

[1]*Future Shock*, pp. 350–351 (1970 edition).

about their products and services, the information that they're gathering tends to be deceptive and useless.

In the same study, 61 to 70 percent of reps felt that buyers aren't relying on salespeople for information before making a purchase and that they're entering the sales situation when the decision has already been made. In other words, according to sales professionals (who are in a position to observe buying behavior from a wide range of customers), buyers are increasingly making premature decisions based upon the wrong kind of information.

With the possible exception of dedicated purchasing agents, very few buyers are either capable of, or interested in, learning enough information to make an informed decision about a product and service area that's outside their expertise. What's far more common is the buyer who merely thinks he or she is educated, when in fact the buyer has simply learned enough to be dangerous. Typically the buyer ends up making a premature decision with inadequate or incorrect information.

Over the next 10 years, cognitive science will debunk the widely touted notion of an educated buyer. The educated buyer will begin to be seen as a liability rather than an asset, and buyers will begin putting even more demand on sales professionals to act as outsourcing managers. Buyers will want sales professionals to provide products and services, without increasing the buyers' own burden of information consumption.

Human Analytics

Human analytics is the extension, both in terms of breadth and depth, of behavioral assessment and skills assessment. Within the next 10 years, new forms of cognitive measurement, cognitive complexity skills, and client fluency will create a new science of human analytics that will give companies the ability to analyze not just the sales results but the makeup of the person creating those results and how those two elements interconnect.

Tools like the PI and the SSAT allow today's sales managers to view an employee or candidate in a more quantifiable and measurable manner, thereby allowing better comparisons, better job placements, increased performance, and better job satisfaction. The future will see additional tools for measuring other aspects of behavior and performance.

An area that's particularly ripe for new research is the effectiveness of online communication tools, like e-mail and social media.

For example, even though social media has become a common tool inside today's sales organizations, there's little consensus (but plenty of opinions) about how it can and should be used for selling. Experts on social media can't even agree on something as simple as how social media should be measured financially. For example, Clara Shih, author of the book *The Facebook Era*, recently admitted to the coauthor of this book "many companies recognize the intrinsic value of engaging with customers and see investing in social networking as a strategic play, much like a website or company e-mail system."

Savvy sales managers—who must deal with making quarterly numbers—tend to rightly be skeptical of any technology that is supposed to have a value that's intrinsic or strategic, without being measurably tied to the actual generation of revenue. This skepticism may account for the reluctance of sales organizations to get sales reps personally trained on social media. As a sales manager from Microsoft (!) said in a meeting attended by the coauthor: "Frankly, I don't want my reps wasting half their day screwing around on Facebook."

This dilemma over the proper usage of social media echoes the problems that companies have encountered with e-mail. In 2007, the *New York Times* described e-mail as "a $650 Billion Drag on the Economy" and in 2011 MSNBC quoted statistics suggesting that six times more e-mails were sent in 2011 than just two years previously. Salespeople are reeling. In a recent study by Ogilvyone, as many as 84 percent of the reps surveyed believe that being a sales rep will be radically different in five years, largely because of the introduction of new technology.

As social media is added to existing tools, like web conferencing and e-mail, scientists will need better and more comprehensive forms of human analytics to fully understand where such technology is effective in building customer relationships and where it falls short. This demand for a scientific approach to cost/benefit will emerge from the understandable unwillingness of sales managers (and companies in general) to continue to invest in technology based on vague promises of greater productivity.

There will similarly be increased research on the effectiveness of distance learning versus face-to-face learning, self-paced learning versus instructor-led learning, and individual class learning versus group learning. Right now, there's a trend away from the physical classroom and toward a virtual classroom using various forms of e-learning, a shift being driven largely by economics.

The application of human analytics, however, would allow that shift to be driven (or balked) by a better understanding of what's actually effective in terms of changing behavior. For example, in September of 2009, the Aberdeen Group, a respected research organization, published research from over 500 companies strongly suggesting that the most effective way to do sales training is through in-person, face-to-face training. Among all companies that deploy external training solutions, those favoring instructor-led methodologies show an average 14 percent increase in the percentage of sales reps achieving their annual quota.

Predictive Analytics

Predictive analytics is a branch of statistics that uses modeling, data mining, and game theory to analyze current and historical facts, in order to make predictions about future events.

In business, predictive models are already being used to exploit patterns in historical and transactional data to identify risks and opportunities. These models capture relationships among many factors to allow assessment of risk or potential associated with a particular set of conditions guiding decision making.

Predictive analytics is also heavily used in actuarial science, financial services, insurance, retail, travel, telecommunications, health care, pharmaceuticals, and other fields. Possibly the best known application is credit scoring, used throughout the financial services industry to rank-order individuals based on their likelihood of making future credit payments on time.

Predictive models are currently being used to analyze past buying behaviors and sales performance in order to assess how likely a customer is to exhibit a specific behavior in the future. Such models can also answer questions about customer performance, such as evaluate the risk or opportunity of a given customer or transaction, in order to guide the application of sales resources to that opportunity.

As computers continue to grow faster, modeling systems will be able to better simulate human behavior and reaction to given stimuli or scenarios. It thus becomes possible to quantify relationships in data in a way that is often used to classify customers or prospects into groups, for better use in targeting marketing and sales campaigns to specific demographics of prospects and customers.

Predictive analysis is also being applied to CRM data in order to create a holistic view of the customer no matter where their information resides in the company or the department involved. Such tools allow a company to posture and focus their efforts effectively across the breadth of their customer base. They make it possible to predict a customer's buying habits in order to promote relevant products at multiple touch points, and proactively identify and mitigate issues that have the potential to lose customers or reduce their ability to gain new ones.

For instance, Professor Oldroyd recently examined and analyzed the electronic logs of more than a million cold calls, made by thousands of sales professionals inside approximately 50 companies. By analyzing that data using algorithms that predict the spread of infectious diseases, he discovered which days and times are most effective for qualifying a sales lead, and who accesses a website into a real prospect that belongs in the pipeline (e.g., Thursday is 19.1 percent better than Friday.).

Neuroscience

Neuroscience (aka neurobiology) is the study of the nervous system. It is an interdisciplinary science that collaborates with other fields such as chemistry, computer science, engineering, linguistics, mathematics, medicine and allied disciplines, philosophy, physics, and psychology.

The scope of neuroscience includes different approaches used to study the molecular, cellular, developmental, structural, functional, evolutionary, computational, and medical aspects of the nervous system. The techniques used by neuroscientists have also expanded enormously, from molecular and cellular studies of individual nerve cells to imaging of sensory and motor tasks in the brain.

Neuroscience opens up entire vistas for scientifically studying the behaviors of both buyers and sellers. For example, sales negotiations sometimes involve bluffing, both on the part of the buyer and the seller. A recent study conducted by Meghana A. Bhatt, a fellow at Baylor College of Medicine's department of neuroscience used brains scans to determine how people's minds work when they're trying to get somebody else to believe something that's not true.

The study monitored the brains of 76 volunteers who took part in a bargaining game between a buyer and a seller. Scans of the participant's brains during the game revealed that there was a "very significant difference in brain responses" between those who bluffed and those who didn't, according to the study's coauthor Read Montague. Similar studies will undoubtedly be conducted on other aspects of the buyer-seller relationship, possibly leading to a greater understanding of how the brain works during business transactions.

Another fertile area for research will be the role that different parts of the brain play in the decision-making process. According to neuroscientist Paul D. MacLean, the human brain has a triune structure consisting of three parts:

- A Reptilian Brain. This part of the brain originally dominated the forebrains of reptiles and birds. The reptilian brain is responsible for instinctual behaviors involved in aggression, dominance, territoriality, ritual displays, and the fight or flight decision in response to danger.
- The Limbic System. This is the part of the brain that arose early in mammalian evolution and is believed to be responsible for the motivation and emotion involved in feeding, reproductive behavior, and parental behavior. It influences the endocrine system (hormones, essentially) and the autonomic nervous system and some scientists contend it is the source of the pleasure obtained from solving problems, a common occurrence in buyer/seller relationships.
- The Neocortex. This is also a structure found uniquely in mammals, but it is massively larger (proportionately) in humans than in other mammals. It is seen as the most recent step in the evolution of the human brain, conferring the ability for language, abstraction, planning, and perception.

The neocortex is itself separated into two halves or hemispheres. The brain architectures, types of cells, types of neurotransmitters, and receptor subtypes are all distributed among the two hemispheres in a markedly asymmetric fashion.

The left hemisphere is primarily concerned with linear reasoning functions of language such as grammar and word production, numerical computation (exact calculation, numerical comparison, estimation), and direct fact retrieval.

The right hemisphere is primarily concerned with the holistic reasoning functions of language such as intonation and emphasis, approximate calculations and estimations, as well as pragmatic and contextual understanding (i.e., common sense).

This is of importance to selling and sales behavior because scanning different parts of the brain, during the decision-making process, may be able to reveal, in a measurable and reproducible way, exactly how buyers make decisions and in response to different types of stimulae provided by a sales professional.

Science will thus begin to alter the ways that sales professionals approach selling situations. For example, a sales team might discover that a presentation starting with the top 12 reasons a company should do business with a rep (thereby appealing to the left hemisphere of the neocortex) may be less effective than a presentation beginning with a personal story about the rep (appealing more to the right hemisphere and the limbic system).

The key point here is that neuroscience may provide a scientific way to measure what kinds of sales interventions (training, coaching, mentoring) behaviors are *actually* effective, as opposed to what is (usually anecdotally) *assumed* to be effective.

A Final Word

The advent of real science into the business of selling is creating a true revolution in both selling itself and the management of sales professionals.

Scientific selling offers sales leaders an alternative to management by gut, an alternative that is accurate, predictable, and reproducible. With scientific selling, sales managers can analyze a job, hire for success, motivate for sustainable results, understand team dynamics, leverage the strengths of each individual, ameliorate the weaknesses, and coach each sales employee to achieve the highest possible level of performance.

Science selling extracts the mystery from the questions that have plagued sales managers since the dawn of selling as a specific job category. It is no longer necessary to guess, based upon instinct, why top producers perform better than average ones, or how average performers can improve. Armed with scientific data, sales leaders can give both the team, and each individual in the team, exactly what's needed to get the best possible results.

The future is bright as well from the perspective of the sales employee. Because science extracts much of the mystery of selling, it becomes a career with a much more predictable future, especially for those who treat it like a profession. Scientific selling increases the value of the individual to the organization, and drives more and more intelligent investing in sales education and sales tools. It creates rigor where before there was dogma.

Scientific selling also means change and sometimes that change may be painful. Old ideas die hard, especially when people are accustomed to believe that those ideas are self-evident. Even so, the advantages of shedding these ancient sales superstitions are that sales managers, teams, and individuals will be able to truly excel in their marketplace, become more competitive and, ultimately, have a greater and more lasting impact on the business world.

Index

212

Index

Crisis in sales management, 6–13

Criterion-related validity, 183, 189

Cross-cultural aspects of sales coaching, 105–108

CSO Insights, 6, 7, 50

Customer-Centric Selling (Bosworth), 41

Customer-Focused Selling (CFS), 41–42, 44, 48, 148–150

  applying the investigate skill stage, 159–162

  applying the open skill stage, 150–158

  applying the confirm skill stage, 165–170

  applying the present skill stage, 162–165

  using the position skill stage, 170–172

Customer Relationship Management (CRM), 5, 10–11, 40, 121, 122–124

Customized training, 83, 85–87

D

Daniels, Arnold S., 30, 32

Data mining, 204

DDI, 29

Death of a Salesman (Miller), 73

Decision making, 185

Deloitte LLP, 8, 9, 10, 117, 118

Demographics, 183–184

  PI, 190–191

  SSAT, 194–195

Diagnostic questions, 43

Dominance, 127, 184

Drucker, Peter, 37

E

Eades, Keith, 47

Eastwood, Mike, 142–144

Educated buyers, 201–202

Effectiveness of behavioral assessment, 27–28

80/20 rule, 7, 50

E-mail, 203

Employee(s). *See also* Sales representatives

  happiness and satisfaction, 137

  importance of upward career paths for, 120–121

  motivation and behavioral science, 23

  paths for advancement in leadership roles, 137

  retention and behavioral science, 26

  in the right jobs, 119–120

  turnover rates, 7–10, 50–51, 116–118

  understanding and appreciating, 136–137

Enterprise Bank, 35

Entrepreneurship, 21–22

  building a culture of innovation and, 124

  fostering, 129–133

Equitable Life Assurance, 46

Ernst and Young, 21, 120, 130

ES Research, 8–9, 10, 71

Execution scenario in sales coaching, 101

Exford, Dorrin, 89–91

"Expectancy Theory," 32–33

Expressers (social style), 152–157

Extroversion, 127, 184–185

F

Facebook, 21, 203

Facebook Era, The (Shih), 203

Feedback, job, 24

Fields, W. C., 73

Filtering of résumés, 60–62

Findings, reviewing, 87

First Nonprofit Insurance Company, 109–110

Ford Motor Company, 46

Formality, 128, 185

G

Game theory, 204

Gartner Group, 10, 123

Gates, Bill, 21

Generations and turnover rates, 9, 117–118

Genetics, 20, 33

Gladwell, Malcolm, 54

Glengarry Glen Ross, 74

Globalization of selling, 5

Goals, 20, 33

Godbout, Andrew, 96–98

Goldenberg, Barton, 11

Golf Ventures West, 142–144

Greatest Salesman in the World, The, 47

H

Hackman, Richard, 33

Handy, Jam, 73

Harris, Todd, 7, 50, 181

Herran, Andrea, 67, 69

Herzberg, Frederick, 32